DR. SEBI HERBAL BIBLE

3 BOOKS IN 1

The Complete Guide to Harness Dr. Sebi's Healing Herbs
for Deep Body Cleansing and Lifelong Vitality

Valeria-Cruz Mendez

Table of Contents

A Message for You

My story began in the heart of the Amazon Rainforest, where the symphony of nature plays its endless melody. I am Valeria Cruz-Mendez, born under the canopy of Brazil's lush jungles, in a small village near Manaus. My childhood was a tapestry woven with the vibrant threads of traditional folklore and the rich biodiversity surrounding us. Yet, in the irony of life, it was not here, but in the sterile corridors of hospitals, that my true journey would begin.

I remember vividly the day my health faltered. It was a humid summer afternoon in 1995, and I was only 30. What started as a minor ailment spiraled into a relentless battle with chronic illness. Over the next decade, I became a living testament to the limitations of modern medicine. Despite the best efforts of esteemed doctors in São Paulo and Rio de Janeiro, my condition only worsened. I was entangled in a cycle of potent pharmaceuticals, each leaving its mark on my already frail body. By 2005, I was a mere 45 kilograms, plagued by constant fatigue and a sense of hopelessness.

It was during these darkest moments that Dr. Sebi's teachings found me. A friend, moved by my plight, introduced me to his holistic approach. Skeptical yet desperate, I delved into his work. I learned about the body's natural alkalinity and the healing powers of a plant-based diet. Dr. Sebi's philosophy, rooted in the African Bio-Mineral Balance, was a revelation. It proposed a diet devoid of hybrid foods, non-natural sugars, and artificial additives – starkly contrasting my previous eating habits. Embracing this new lifestyle was like emerging from a long, dark tunnel. Slowly, the vitality I thought was lost forever began to return. Within a year, my weight normalized, and the debilitating symptoms that had shadowed my existence receded. By 2007, I was not just surviving; I was thriving. My transformation was not just physical but spiritual too. I reconnected with the wisdom of my ancestors and the healing power of the Amazon's herbs and plants that I had known as a child.

This book is a culmination of my journey and a tribute to the wisdom that saved me. I dedicate it to the weary souls who have been let down by conventional paths and seek refuge in the embrace of nature. It is for those who believe in the harmony of the body, mind, and spirit. Let my story be a testament to the power of natural healing and a guide to those who seek a path back to wellness. As you turn these pages, remember that every word is infused with my experiences, struggles, and triumphs. The *"Dr. Sebi Herbal Bible"* is not just a collection of teachings; it is a beacon of hope, a map for those lost in the labyrinth of modern medicine, and a reminder that sometimes the cure we seek lies in the roots of nature itself. Welcome to a journey of rediscovery, healing, and empowerment.

INTRODUCTION

My dear reader, welcome to the *"Dr. Sebi Herbal Bible,"* a comprehensive guide designed to immerse you in the holistic healing pioneered by Dr. Sebi. This book is an invitation to explore the philosophy and practices of a man who dedicated his life to unlocking the healing potential of nature. Our journey through these pages will uncover the core principles and philosophies underpinning Dr. Sebi's unique approach to health and wellness. The heart of this guide lies in its detailed exploration of a range of holistic herbal remedies, all inspired by Dr. Sebi's teachings.

These remedies are meticulously crafted to target specific body systems, promoting overall health and vitality. You will learn about the healing properties of herbs like burdock root, dandelion, and bladderwrack, and discover how to prepare these potent natural medicines at home. *"The Dr. Sebi Herbal Bible"* goes beyond being a mere compendium of ancient natural wisdom; it's an actionable guide to integrating these time-tested practices into your everyday life, enhancing your health and wellbeing. It encourages a deeper appreciation of the natural world and its profound ability to nurture and heal us.

As we navigate the chapters of this book, we pay homage to Dr. Sebi's lifelong commitment to uncovering the truth about natural healing and promoting a holistic lifestyle. This book is a clarion call to those who seek more than just knowledge and aspire for a life of holistic well-being. Whether you are beginning to explore the wonders of herbal medicine or are a seasoned practitioner, these pages offer inspiration and empowerment. Join us in celebrating Dr. Sebi's legacy, and discover the incredible power of nature to heal and transform. Let this book guide you to a healthier, more vibrant life, rooted in the timeless wisdom of nature's healing touch.

BOOK 1: UNDERSTANDING HOLISTIC HERBAL WELLNESS

CHAPTER 1

INTRODUCTION TO DR. SEBI'S HERBAL PHILOSOPHY

In the heart of Mother Nature's verdant embrace lies a silent, powerful rhythm of healing, waiting to be discovered. One such seeker who ventured into the dense foliage of the unknown and emerged with a treasure trove of herbal wisdom was Dr. Sebi. Through this chapter, we embark on the journey to unearth the philosophy of healing that Dr. Sebi propounded, a philosophy that is as profound as it is transformative.

Dr. Sebi, born Alfredo Bowman in the verdant lap of Honduras in 1933, was more than just a healer; he was a harbinger of holistic wellness in a world fixated on symptomatic treatment. His essence resonated with the ancient rhythms of nature, a resonance that guided him beyond the veil of conventional medicine and into the heart of nature's timeless wisdom. As a self-educated man, his quest for knowledge was unquenchable, leading him to unfurl the holistic philosophy that now bears his name. His eyes, unclouded by the conventional paradigms, saw the profound interconnectedness between the human body and the natural world. His vision pierced through the symptomatic understanding of diseases, diving deep into the essence of holistic wellness, which he believed was attainable by embracing nature's boundless offerings. His life was a living testament to an age-old belief, a belief that nature, in her boundless wisdom and generosity, has provided a healing balm for every malaise that afflicts the human body and soul.

At the core of Dr. Sebi's herbal philosophy lay a pristine purity that mirrored the untouched, verdant forests where herbs grew in wild abundance. His was an unyielding faith in the healing power of herbs, a faith rooted in an intimate understanding of nature's rhythm and balance. He revered the natural world, seeing in every leaf and herb a potential key to unlock the doors of wellness that modern medicine often found elusive. His holistic approach transcended the physicality of healing, reaching into the soul, seeking to restore a harmonious balance that modern lifestyles had disrupted. Dr. Sebi's philosophy was a clarion call to return to our roots, rekindle a harmonious relationship with nature, and nourish our bodies with a natural alkaline diet, which he propounded as the cornerstone of health and vitality. His belief was simple yet profound; aligning one's diet and lifestyle with the alkaline design of the body could usher in a state of wellness that transcended the physical, mental, and emotional realms.

Dr. Sebi envisioned a world where individuals could reclaim control over their health, empowered by the knowledge and the herbal tools nature generously provided. His approach was not about waging a war against diseases, but about nurturing the body's inherent ability to heal, about restoring the lost equilibrium that was the root cause of disorders. His herbal philosophy was a voyage back to a time when healing was a holistic endeavor, when herbs were revered as sacred keys to wellness, when the body was seen not as a machine to be fixed, but as a part of the grand tapestry of nature, deserving of nurturing and holistic care.

Dr. Sebi's journey from a self-healer to a holistic healer of many is a narrative of self-discovery, a relentless quest for truth in the verdant lap of nature, and a life lived in service to humanity's wellness. His life and philosophy invite us to embark on our journey of self-discovery, to seek wellness not just in eradicating symptoms but in the holistic vitality that comes from living in harmony with nature's profound wisdom. Through the lens of Dr. Sebi's herbal philosophy, we are ushered into a realm where every herb is a note in a grand symphony. This symphony can restore the body's lost harmony and usher in holistic wellness. Dr. Sebi's exploration into the heart of herbal wisdom was not just a scholarly endeavor, but a personal quest. His journey began with his own battle against ailments, leaving him seeking answers beyond the confines of modern medicine. The answers he found were not in synthetic concoctions but in the unadulterated essence of herbs.

He propounded the belief that mucus was the precursor to many diseases and by adopting an alkaline diet rich in natural herbs, one could achieve a state of wellness. This was not just a theory but a lived reality for Dr. Sebi, whose vitality bore testimony to the truth of his teachings. Dr. Sebi's teachings invite us to view herbs as a means to alleviate symptoms and as a pathway to holistic wellness. Each herb, in his view, is a note in a divine symphony, a symphony that can bring about a profound transformation in our state of being when played in harmony. Dr. Sebi demystified herbal medicine in his lifetime, making it accessible to individuals far and wide. His approach was not to wage a war against diseases but to nurture the inherent ability of the body to heal, to restore the lost equilibrium.

As we delve deeper into Dr. Sebi's herbal philosophy in the ensuing chapters, we will explore the myriad herbs he championed, the principles of the alkaline diet he advocated, and the essence of a lifestyle in tune with nature's rhythm. His philosophy is a beacon for those weary of the cacophony of modern-day medical maze, a soothing melody guiding towards a state of natural wellness. Dr. Sebi's legacy is not just a collection of herbal remedies; it's an invitation to embrace a life of vibrant health, embark on a voyage of self-discovery through the gentle whispers of herbs, and live in harmony with Mother Nature's ancient, wise rhythm. Thus begins our journey into the heart of Dr. Sebi's herbal wisdom, which promises healing and a profound understanding of the intrinsic bond between nature and the self. Through the pages of this book, may the essence of Dr. Sebi's profound wisdom seep into the realms of your consciousness, inspiring a transformation that resonates with the natural rhythm of existence.

Core Principles of Dr. Sebi's Alkaline Diet

Embarking on the path of Dr. Sebi's alkaline diet is akin to returning to an ancient, natural way of living, one that seeks to align our bodies with the inherent design of nature. Dr. Sebi, a beacon of wisdom in holistic wellness, presented to the world a simple yet profound truth: the alkaline nature of our body is the cornerstone of health and vitality. His alkaline diet is not a mere dietary regimen, but a philosophy of living in harmony with nature's rhythm. In this chapter, we delve into the core principles that form the bedrock of Dr. Sebi's alkaline diet, unveiling a path of wellness that is as profound as transformative.

1. **Alkaline Versus Acidic Foods:** Dr. Sebi's alkaline diet hinges on the understanding that our body's natural state is alkaline, and maintaining this alkalinity is crucial for optimal health. He emphasized the importance of consuming alkaline foods and herbs that support this natural state, while avoiding acidic foods that disrupt it. As per Dr. Sebi, alkaline foods are natural, unprocessed, and free from synthetic chemicals.

2. **Cellular Nourishment:** Central to Dr. Sebi's philosophy is the belief that nourishing the cell is the key to healing and wellness. He propounded that diseases arise when the cells are deprived of nourishment and the alkaline diet is a means to ensure that every cell is adequately nourished and cleansed.

3. **Natural and Electric Foods:** Dr. Sebi revered what he termed 'electric foods' foods that are not just alkaline but also natural and unaltered by hybridization or genetic modification. These foods, he believed, are high in mineral content and electric energy, vital for the optimal functioning and healing of the human body.

4. **Elimination of Mucus:** Dr. Sebi often said mucus is the root cause of many diseases. An alkaline diet, rich in natural, electric foods, aids in eliminating mucus from the body, restoring the natural balance and wellness.

5. **Fasting and Detoxification:** Fasting and detoxification are integral to Dr. Sebi's alkaline diet. He believed fasting, when combined with the consumption of herbal teas and alkaline foods, can significantly aid in detoxifying the body and rejuvenating the cells.

6. **Herbal Healing:** Herbs are significant in Dr. Sebi's alkaline diet. He was a strong proponent of using herbs for healing diseases, daily nourishment, and health maintenance.
7. **Simplicity and Natural Living:** Simplicity is a hallmark of Dr. Sebi's alkaline diet. He advocated a simple, natural lifestyle that is in harmony with nature. This includes consuming a simple diet rich in natural, alkaline, and electric foods, and leading a stress-free life attuned to nature's rhythm.

Dr. Sebi's alkaline diet is a pathway to rediscovering a state of wellness often lost in modern living. It invites us to strip away the complexities, return to a way of living that is in tune with the natural order, and nourish our bodies with nature's pure, alkaline essence. Through the lens of Dr. Sebi's alkaline diet, we are ushered into a realm where wellness is not a distant dream but a lived reality, attainable through the gentle embrace of nature's profound wisdom.

The Impact of an Alkaline Body: Prevention and Healing

Dr. Sebi, a venerated holistic healer, bestowed upon the world a treasure trove of wisdom encapsulated in his alkaline diet philosophy. He elucidated a profound yet simple truth; the state of our body's pH can be the compass guiding us towards a haven of health or a precipice of ailments. According to Dr. Sebi, the alkaline realm is where the body's healing prowess is at its zenith.

1. **Prevention of Chronic Diseases:** The cornerstone of Dr. Sebi's alkaline diet is the prevention of diseases. He posited that an alkaline body creates an inhospitable terrain for diseases, keeping chronic ailments like diabetes, heart disease, and cancer at bay. By nurturing an alkaline state, one fortifies the body's natural defenses, thwarting the incursion of disease-causing entities.
2. **Boosting Immunity:** Dr. Sebi propounded that an alkaline body is synonymous with a robust immune system. The alkaline diet, rich in natural, mineral-dense foods, fortifies the immune fortresses, enabling the body to gallantly fend off infections and illnesses, maintaining a state of vibrant health.
3. **Enhanced Cellular Function and Repair:** At the cellular level, Dr. Sebi's alkaline diet aims to nurture a conducive environment for cellular vigor. He believed that an alkaline body ensures optimal cellular function and augments the body's self-repair mechanisms, keeping the specter of diseases at a distance.
4. **Detoxification and Elimination of Mucus:** Dr. Sebi often underscored that an alkaline body is detoxified. The alkaline diet, he postulated, facilitates the elimination of mucus

and toxins, which he identified as the precursors of numerous ailments. The body reclaims its natural equilibrium through detoxification, setting the stage for healing and rejuvenation.

5. **Promotion of Mental Clarity and Well-being:** The tendrils of the alkaline diet, according to Dr. Sebi, extend into the realms of mental and emotional well-being. An alkaline body fosters mental clarity, nurtures a serene mind, and cultivates a fertile ground for positive thoughts and emotions to flourish.

6. **Herbal Healing:** Dr. Sebi revered the healing prowess of herbs. He curated a repertoire of herbs that complement the alkaline diet, working in symphony to sustain an alkaline body and facilitate healing. His herbal formulations are seen as the conduits through which nature imparts its healing touch.

7. **Longevity and Anti-aging:** Pursuing longevity and a vibrant life is at the heart of Dr. Sebi's alkaline diet. By promoting an alkaline body, he believed, one could slow the aging process and revel in a life of vitality regardless of age.

Dr. Sebi's alkaline diet is a beacon for those seeking a natural pathway to health, a life less encumbered by ailments, and a fulfilling existence in harmony with nature's laws. Through his teachings, Dr. Sebi invites us to traverse this path, to explore the boundless potential of an alkaline body in fostering prevention and healing, and to embrace a life of wellness that resonates with the natural order of existence.

CHAPTER 2

THE POWER OF ALKALINE HERBS

Definition and Benefits of Alkaline Herbs

In Dr. Sebi's holistic health philosophy, alkaline herbs are venerable, acting as the botanical keys to unlock a cascade of healing energies within the body. These herbs, known for their alkaline nature, are believed to resonate with the body's inherent alkaline state, fostering a harmonious balance that is quintessential for optimal health and wellness. Alkaline herbs grow in natural, untampered soils, basking in the purity of Mother Nature, and are believed to hold a higher degree of electrical resonance that aligns with the human body. They are revered for their ability to restore the body's alkaline balance, disrupted by the consumption of acidic foods and exposure to environmental toxins. Here are the benefits of alkaline herbs:

1. **Restoration of Alkaline Balance:** The paramount benefit of alkaline herbs, according to Dr. Sebi, is their ability to restore the body's alkaline balance. Through their alkaline nature, these herbs help neutralize the acidic waste, promoting an environment where wellness thrives.

2. **Detoxification:** Alkaline herbs are believed to possess potent detoxifying properties. They aid in purging the body of toxins and mucus, which Dr. Sebi identified as the harbinger of diseases.

3. **Cellular Nourishment and Repair:** The mineral-rich composition of alkaline herbs nourishes the cells. Dr. Sebi emphasized that the mineral balance is crucial for cellular vitality, and alkaline herbs play a pivotal role in replenishing minerals and fostering cellular repair.

4. **Immune System Fortification:** By promoting an alkaline environment and providing a bounty of essential minerals, alkaline herbs contribute to fortifying the immune system, making it more adept at warding off infections and diseases.

5. **Anti-inflammatory Properties:** Many alkaline herbs possess anti-inflammatory properties, crucial in alleviating inflammation, a common precursor to numerous chronic diseases.

6. **Enhanced Digestive Health:** Alkaline herbs also improve digestive health by promoting a balanced pH level in the digestive tract, aiding in eliminating waste, and nurturing a healthy gut flora.

7. **Mental Clarity and Emotional Well-being:** The holistic benefits of alkaline herbs extend to mental and emotional well-being. By fostering a balanced internal environment, these herbs contribute to mental clarity and a serene emotional state, according to Dr. Sebi's teachings.

8. **Longevity and Vitality:** The cumulative effect of the above benefits contributes to enhanced longevity and vitality. By adhering to a lifestyle replete with alkaline herbs, individuals can traverse the aging process with grace and vitality, as proposed by Dr. Sebi.

Alkaline herbs emerge as indispensable allies in the quest for holistic health and longevity through their inherent purity and resonance with the body's natural state. They are the botanical embodiments of Dr. Sebi's philosophy, offering a natural conduit through which individuals can rekindle a harmonious dialogue with nature, and traverse the path of healing with a heart full of hope and a body brimming with life.

Alkaline Herbs vs. Other Herbs

In botanicals, herbs emerge as the cornerstone of traditional healing practices, each with unique properties. Among them, alkaline herbs hold a distinctive position, especially within Dr. Sebi's holistic health philosophy. This section aims to delineate the contrasts between alkaline herbs advocated by Dr. Sebi, and other herbs that may not align with the alkaline doctrine.

1. Origin and Growth

Alkaline Herbs: Alkaline herbs are often indigenous, grown in untouched, pristine soils free from synthetic chemicals and genetic modification. They thrive in environments that mirror their natural habitats, allowing them to absorb the minerals and nutrients that contribute to their alkaline nature.

Other Herbs: Other herbs may be cultivated in controlled or modified environments, possibly using synthetic fertilizers, pesticides, or genetic engineering to enhance certain traits, which might alter their natural alkaline or acidic balance.

2. Alkalinity vs. Acidity

Alkaline Herbs: Dr. Sebi's alkaline herbs are characterized by their ability to support the body's natural alkaline state, essential for optimal health and disease prevention.

Other Herbs: Other herbs might possess a range of pH levels, some being acidic, which may not support the body's alkaline balance as per Dr. Sebi's teachings.

3. Mineral Content

Alkaline Herbs: Alkaline herbs are revered for their high mineral content, which is fundamental to cellular nourishment, according to Dr. Sebi.

Other Herbs: The mineral content in other herbs may vary, and might not align with the mineral profile advocated by Dr. Sebi for optimal health.

4. Electrical Resonance

Alkaline Herbs: Dr. Sebi often emphasized the electrical resonance of alkaline herbs, believing that they possess a higher degree of electrical energy vital for the body's healing and vitality.

Other Herbs: The concept of electrical resonance might not be a recognized or emphasized characteristic in other herbs outside of Dr. Sebi's teachings.

5. Healing Properties

Alkaline Herbs: The healing properties of alkaline herbs as stated by Dr. Sebi encompass detoxification, immune support, inflammation reduction, and overall promotion of an alkaline body conducive to healing.

Other Herbs: Other herbs may possess a wide array of healing properties recognized in various traditional or modern medicinal practices, which may or may not focus on alkalinity as a central healing principle.

6. Integration in Diet

Alkaline Herbs: Alkaline herbs are integral to Dr. Sebi's dietary guidelines, forming a harmonious synergy with the alkaline diet for holistic wellness.

Other Herbs: Other herbs might not have specific dietary guidelines and may be incorporated into various dietary practices without emphasizing alkalinity.

7. Recognition and Adoption

Alkaline Herbs: Adopting alkaline herbs is central to those following Dr. Sebi's teachings and others who subscribe to the alkaline diet philosophy.

Other Herbs: Other herbs enjoy a wide recognition and adoption across various traditional and modern medicinal practices, irrespective of their pH level.

The comparative exploration elucidates the distinctive essence of alkaline herbs in alignment with Dr. Sebi's holistic health philosophy. These herbs, through their alkaline nature and other unique attributes, resonate with the principles of natural living and holistic healing as Dr. Sebi propagates, offering a unique path to wellness distinct from the broader spectrum of herbal   remedies.

List of Approved Dr. Sebi Herbs

The following is a list of Dr. Sebi approved alkaline herbs along with a brief description of their properties as per his teachings:

1. *Arnica:* Known for its pain-relieving and anti-inflammatory properties.
2. *Batana Oil:* Often used for hair and skin care.
3. *Black Walnut Hull:* Known for its antifungal and antiparasitic benefits.
4. *Bladderwrack:* A seaweed rich in minerals, particularly iodine, often used for thyroid support.
5. *Blessed Thistle:* Known for supporting digestion and treating liver and gallbladder disorders.
6. *Blue Vervain:* Often used for its calming and mood-enhancing properties.
7. *Bugleweed:* Known for its ability to support thyroid health.
8. *Burdock Root:* Recognized for its blood purifying and skin healing properties.
9. *Cascara Sagrada:* Often used as a natural laxative.
10. *Chamomile:* Known for its calming effects and ability to support sleep.
11. *Chaparral:* Recognized for its antioxidant and antiviral properties.
12. *Cocolmeca:* Known for its blood purifying properties.
13. *Contribo:* Traditionally used for digestive ailments.
14. *Cordoncillo Negro:* Known for its anti-inflammatory and analgesic properties.
15. *Damiana:* Often used as a mood enhancer and aphrodisiac.
16. *Dandelion Root:* Recognized for its liver detoxifying properties.
17. *Elderberry:* Known for its immune-boosting properties, particularly during colds and flu.
18. *Eucalyptus:* Known for its antiseptic and respiratory benefits.
19. *Eyebright:* Traditionally used for eye health.
20. *Flor De Manita:* Traditionally used for heart conditions.
21. *Guaco:* Known for its expectorant and anti-asthmatic properties.
22. *Guinea Hen Weed:* Recognized for its anti-inflammatory and analgesic properties.
23. *Huereque:* Traditionally used for managing blood sugar levels.
24. *Hombre Grande:* Known for its antiparasitic properties.
25. *Hops:* Often used for its calming effects and sleep support.
26. *Hydrangea Root:* Known for its urinary tract benefits.

27. *Kalawalla:* Recognized for its immune-modulating properties.

28. *Lavender:* Known for its calming and relaxing properties.

29. *Lily of the Valley:* Traditionally used for heart conditions.

30. *Muicle:* Known for its blood purifying properties.

31. *Mullein:* Known for its respiratory benefits, particularly in soothing mucus membranes.

32. *Nettle:* Recognized for its anti-inflammatory properties and ability to support joint health.

33. *Nopal Cactus:* Known for its blood sugar regulating properties.

34. *Prodigiosa:* Traditionally used for blood sugar regulation.

35. *Red Clover:* Known for its blood purifying and skin healing properties.

36. *Rhubarb Root:* Often used as a natural laxative.

37. *Sage:* Known for its antioxidant and cognitive support properties.

38. *Santa Maria:* Traditionally used for pain relief.

39. *Sea Moss:* Known for its high mineral content and ability to support respiratory health.

40. *Sensitiva:* Traditionally used for its calming properties.

41. *Soursop:* Known for its immune-boosting properties.

42. *Tila (Linden Flower):* Often used for its calming and sleep-supporting properties.

43. *Valerian:* Known for its ability to support sleep and reduce anxiety.

44. *Yellow Dock:* Recognized for its blood purifying properties.

45. *Yohimbe:* Traditionally used as an aphrodisiac and for enhancing circulation.

CHAPTER 3

DETOXIFICATION AND CELLULAR CLEANSING

The human body is constantly exposed to toxins from the environment, diet, and lifestyle. These toxins can build up in the body and lead to various health problems. Detoxification is the process of removing harmful substances from the body. This can be achieved through dietary changes, physical activities, and natural remedies such as herbal cleanses. The benefits of detoxification include improved energy levels, mental clarity, immune system function, weight loss, and overall well-being.

1. Improved Energy Levels: One of the significant benefits of detoxification is increased energy levels. Toxins can negatively affect our energy production across cells by disrupting cellular metabolism. By cleansing the body of these harmful substances, you allow your cells to function optimally, increasing energy production. This improved energy flow helps support physical activity, mental focus, and overall vitality.

2. Mental Clarity: Toxins can interfere with neurological processes in the brain, which may result in reduced cognitive function. Detoxification helps clear these toxins from neurotransmitters and other brain parts linked to memory and concentration. As a result, you may experience better mental clarity, improved memory retention, enhanced problem-solving abilities, and even a reduced risk of developing neurodegenerative diseases such as Alzheimer's later in life.

3. Enhanced Immune System Function: Removing toxins from your body supports the optimal function of your immune system. A healthy immune system is vital in preventing illnesses and infections caused by bacteria or viruses — defending you against potentially severe or deadly diseases. By detoxifying your body regularly through Dr. Sebi's Herbal Cleanses or incorporating detoxifying foods into your diet, you help to keep your immune system robust and functioning properly.

4. Weight Loss: Detoxification can also aid in weight loss by helping your body reset and reduce the impact of toxins on hormonal balances related to weight regulation. Moreover, many detox diets are centered around consuming whole, plant-based foods that are naturally lower in calories and high in fiber, promoting weight loss through improved digestion and a faster metabolism.

5. Skin Health: Your skin is your body's largest organ and is a primary barrier between internal organs and the external environment. Toxins from food, water, air pollution, and beauty products can all harm your skin health. Detoxification helps eliminate these harmful substances from your body, leading to clearer and healthier-looking skin.

6. Reduced Inflammation: Chronic inflammation has been linked to numerous severe health conditions, such as heart disease, diabetes, cancer, and autoimmune diseases. Detoxifying the body through natural remedies can help reduce inflammation levels by eliminating free radicals and other harmful substances that contribute to inflammation. This may lower your risk for chronic diseases associated with inflammation.

Dr. Sebi's Guidelines for Effective Detoxing

In this section, we will delve into the wisdom of Dr. Sebi and explore his guidelines for effective detoxing. Detoxification is essential to maintain a balanced and healthy body, mind, and spirit. Dr. Sebi believed that one can attain optimal health and vitality by eliminating toxins and nurturing our bodies with the right nutrients.

1. Diet: The cornerstone of Dr. Sebi's detoxification approach is adhering to a diet rich in natural, alkaline-forming foods. According to Dr. Sebi, consuming alkaline foods helps neutralize acidity within the body and keeps toxins from accumulating in the vital organs. This allows the body to purge these harmful substances more efficiently. He recommends eliminating processed foods and dairy products and limiting animal protein intake for a successful detox. Some key items in Dr. Sebi's Alkaline Food List include walnuts, avocados, tomatoes, hemp seeds, wild rice, quinoa, amaranth greens, mushrooms like oyster and portobello, and a variety of fruits like seeded melons and seeded grapes.

2. Hydration: Drinking ample water throughout the day is essential for efficient internal cleansing. Adequate hydration helps flush out toxins more effectively while promoting overall health and energy levels. Dr. Sebi suggests consuming water with a high pH level — preferably spring water — to encourage alkalinity in the body.

3. Fasting: According to Dr. Sebi, regular fasting allows the body to rest and recover while helping eliminate toxic waste buildup more rapidly. He posited that intermittent fasting allows natural cellular regeneration processes to function optimally.

4. Herbal Detox Programs: One of Dr. Sebi's primary detox modalities involves using specifically designed herb combinations that target particular organs or systems in the body. The herbs eradicate toxins, waste products, and other harmful substances lodged in the body's tissues over time. His popular herbal detox plans include the Full Body Detox, Liver Cleanse, and Kidney Cleanse programs.

5. Exercise: Regular physical activity is vital to successfully implementing Dr. Sebi's detox guidelines. Exercise facilitates effective circulation and improves oxygenation, aiding optimal cleansing and efficient toxin elimination. Additionally, exercise helps reduce stress and promotes mental well-being.

6. Sleep: Adequate rest is essential for supporting your body during detoxification. Dr. Sebi emphasized that the body needs time to rest and repair from daily activities while maximizing detoxification benefits.

7. Emotional Detoxification: Dr. Sebi believed that emotional well-being plays a significant role in overall health, affecting the body at a cellular level. Stress, unresolved trauma, and negative emotions can lead to a buildup of toxins within the body. He advocated incorporating holistic practices such as deep breathing exercises, meditation, or simply spending time in nature to help release emotional toxicity.

8. Mental Detoxification: Dr. Sebi emphasized the importance of maintaining a positive outlook on life through practices such as mindfulness, meditation, gratitude journaling, and affirmations to support mental health during the detoxification process.

9. Social Detoxification: Associating with like-minded individuals who genuinely support your wellness goals is vital in securing ongoing success throughout your detox journey.

Popular Detox Protocols and Herbal Combinations

Various detox protocols and herbal combinations can help the body cleanse itself from harmful toxins, boost metabolic processes, and restore balance. Let's explore popular detox protocols and herbal combinations inspired by Dr. Sebi's philosophy on detoxification and healing.

1. The 7-Day Full Body Detox: The 7-Day Full Body Detox is one of the most popular detox protocols designed to cleanse the entire body systematically. This holistic cleanse targets major organs such as the liver, kidneys, colon, and lungs while promoting improved digestion, increased energy, mental clarity, and weight management. Combining herbs like cascara sagrada, sarsaparilla, dandelion root, burdock root, and elderberry helps facilitate this process by enhancing the body's detoxification abilities.

2. Lymphatic System Cleanse: The lymphatic system collects and eliminates waste products from our body. A well-functioning lymphatic system ensures a strong immune system and healthy skin. Herbal blends including red clover, cleavers, poke root, echinacea purpurea root, and mullein leaf support lymphatic health by promoting efficient detoxification processes in the lymph nodes and boosting immunity against infections.

3. Liver Detox: The liver is our primary organ for filtering toxins from our bloodstream. Ensuring it functions optimally is crucial for maintaining proper digestion and general health. Milk thistle seed extract is a powerful herb known for protecting liver cells from damage caused by free radicals while stimulating the regeneration of new cells. Other potent herbs for liver detoxification include dandelion root, burdock root, schisandra berry extracts or chi-hu extract.

4. Kidney Cleanse: Our kidneys filter waste products from our bloodstream and regulate electrolyte balances to maintain overall balance in the body. A kidney cleanse can help flush toxins, prevent kidney stones, and boost kidney function. The combination of potent healing herbs such as hydrangea root, sarsaparilla root, goldenrod flower, and marshmallow root has been used traditionally for their diuretic properties, which promote the removal of excess water and waste products from the kidneys.

5. Colon Cleanse: A healthy colon ensures efficient elimination of waste products from our body while facilitating nutrient absorption. A colon cleanse is essential in preventing constipation, bloating, and the build-up of harmful bacteria in the gut. Cascara sagrada or buckthorn bark is a commonly used herb for colon cleansing as it is a natural laxative. Other herbs that aid colonic health include aloe vera leaf, slippery elm bark, and fennel seed.

6. Respiratory Detox: Our respiratory system is constantly exposed to various environmental pollutants and pathogens. Detoxifying the lungs and bronchial passages can help us breathe more comfortably while improving overall respiratory health. Combining beneficial herbs like mullein leaf, elecampane root, lungwort leaf, coltsfoot leaf, and pleurisy root supports respiratory detoxification and promotes clear breathing passages.

7. Alkaline Diet: An essential part of Dr. Sebi's approach to healing revolves around consuming an alkaline diet that consists primarily of natural plant-based foods without any artificial chemicals or preservatives. Incorporating alkalizing herbs such as burdock root, sarsaparilla root, sea moss or Irish moss gel, bladderwrack powder, dandelion greens or dandelion tea can aid in detoxification by increasing the body's pH levels and promoting a balanced internal environment for optimal health.

Incorporating these popular detox protocols and herbal combinations into your daily routine will improve your overall health and well-being by helping your body eliminate harmful toxins. It is essential to consult with a professional practitioner familiar with Dr. Sebi's methodology to ensure safety when implementing these detox protocols, as every individual's body has unique requirements.

CHAPTER 4

MIND-BODY CONNECTION IN HERBAL WELLNESS

Understanding The Mind-Body Connection

The mind-body connection refers to the complex interplay between our thoughts, emotions, and physical sensations and how these factors influence our bodies. The mind's influence on our physical health cannot be overstated. Our thoughts and emotions shape every aspect of our lives—from essential functions like breathing and digestion, to more complex behaviors such as sleep patterns, immune function, and stress response. The same holds for our bodies; they too significantly affect our mental state.

Stress is a prime example of the mind-body connection at play. When we experience stress, physically, emotionally, or mentally, it's not just our minds that feel its brunt—our bodies do as well. This manifests in various symptoms such as fatigue, headaches, lowered immune system function, sleep disturbances, and even chronic pain.

Dr. Sebi's herbal approach advocates for an alkaline-electric diet and natural herbal remedies to achieve optimal health. He believed that an alkaline-based diet helped balance what was happening in the body and significantly supported our mental wellness. By following Dr. Sebi's guidelines and incorporating natural herbs into your daily lifestyle, you can take steps towards nurturing your mind-body connection:

1. Fuel your body with an alkaline-electric diet: Consuming a plant-based diet rich in organic whole foods helps neutralize acidity, reduces inflammation, and supports overall physical health. This alkaline-electric diet promotes mental clarity, reduces stress, and fosters emotional stability, which benefits our mind-body connection.

2. Nurture your mental well-being: Along with an alkaline-electric diet, Dr. Sebi's approach emphasizes the importance of nurturing our emotional and mental health. Meditation, deep breathing exercises, mindfulness practices, and cultivating positive relationships all contribute to a strong and balanced mind-body connection.

3. Choose the right herbs: Dr. Sebi's research has resulted in an extensive list of beneficial herbs that possess potent healing properties without introducing harmful substances into the body. You support your physical and mental health by selecting the appropriate herbs based on your needs.

Dr. Sebi recommends several specific herbs for enhancing mind-body wellness:

1. Blue vervain: An excellent herb for reducing stress and anxiety by calming the nervous system.

2. Damiana: A well-known aphrodisiac that not only stimulates sexual energy but also promotes relaxation and elevates mood.

3. Guaco: This herb is useful for improving digestion and soothing inflammation caused by irritated mucus membranes – thus relieving both body and mind.

4. Linden flower: Known for its calming properties, Linden flower helps reduce anxiety levels and assists in dealing with insomnia or restlessness caused by mental stress.

5.Valerian root: This powerful herb is revered for relieving tension headaches, easing anxiety, and decreasing symptoms of stress-related issues such as high blood pressure.

By understanding the significance of the mind-body connection, you can adopt Dr. Sebi's unique herbal approach to transform your holistic wellness journey—achieving harmony between your thoughts, emotions, and physical sensations through the power of nature's gifts.

Achieving Balance with Meditation and Mindfulness

Our modern world is often challenging, filled with distractions, stress, and a constant pursuit of productivity. In this fast-paced environment learning to establish equilibrium within ourselves is essential for emotional, physical, and spiritual well-being. *Dr. Sebi's Herbal Bible* emphasizes the importance of meditation and mindfulness as key instruments in attaining this balance.

Meditation is an ancient practice that involves concentration, relaxation, and self-realization. It enables individuals to reach a more profound understanding of themselves while transcending their thoughts and daily concerns. On the other hand, mindfulness encourages individuals to live in the present moment by paying continuous attention to their thoughts, feelings, sensations, and surroundings without judgment. Integrating both practices into a daily routine can gradually increase tranquility and harmony.

The combination of meditation and mindfulness helps in maintaining inner balance by acknowledging negative emotions such as anger, sadness, or fear instead of repressing them.

These practices can further alleviate anxiety levels by helping individuals better manage or reduce stressors in their lives. Additionally, meditation and mindfulness support the immune system's function by lowering cortisol levels responsible for inflammation-induced diseases.

One of the primary benefits of incorporating meditation and mindfulness into one's life is cultivating time and space for self-exploration. This enables individuals to develop greater clarity regarding their aspirations or issues they must address. Meditation can also foster creativity which is crucial for establishing a serene mental state. However, this practice should not pose a daunting task; even beginners can benefit from allotting fifteen mins daily dedicated solely to this reflective practice. It would be best to find a quiet environment to free you from disturbances during your session.

To begin your practice, gently close your eyes while seated in a firm yet comfortable position. Ensure your posture remains erect without feeling strained, signaling readiness and attentiveness. Breathe deeply and slowly, paying close attention to each inhale and exhale. Observing your breath is an excellent way to remain present and day-to-day stressors before focusing on a focal point, such as a particular sensation, word, or object.

Your mind will inevitably wander during meditation; this is a hallmark of the practice. Should you notice any intrusive thoughts or uneasiness arising, acknowledge these feelings without judgment or resistance. Learn to embrace them as part of your journey towards achieving balance. Shift your focus back to your breath or the point of focus, gently ushering your mind away from unnecessary distraction. Further enhance balance in your life by incorporating mindfulness into your daily routine. Endeavor to cultivate awareness of the present moment by concentrating on specific sensations such as how your feet feel against the ground or how sunlight warms your skin as you stroll outdoors. We can grasp life's beauty and preciousness by shifting our mindset from becoming overwhelmed with past or future concerns.

Another effective way of practicing mindfulness is by introducing simple rituals into our daily routine. A daily walk in nature can stimulate mindfulness while simultaneously offering an opportunity for individuals to savor their surroundings and appreciate every aspect of their environment. Dr. Sebi's approach to achieving balance has continually emphasized combining mindfulness practices alongside his nutritional recommendations and herbal remedies. These parallel practices ensure nourishing an individual's mental, emotional, and physical health, reinforcing strength and resilience. Attaining inner equilibrium may require effort, persistence, and patience in allowing yourself to be present in every situation fully. Embracing various practices like meditation, being mindful during everyday chores, or indulging in nature walks will gradually lead you towards a balanced lifestyle guided by inner peace. By consciously engaging with our thoughts, emotions, and physical sensations, we develop a deeper connection with our true selves – fostering self-awareness and cultivating inner serenity. In addition to following Dr. Sebi's dietary recommendations and herbal remedies, incorporating meditation and mindfulness into one's daily routine can significantly benefit overall wellness, paving the way towards sustainable balance, happiness, and a sense of fulfillment!

CHAPTER 5

TRANSITIONING TO AN HERBAL LIFESTYLE

Assessing Your Current Lifestyle and Health

Transitioning to an herbal lifestyle, particularly one guided by Dr. Sebi's principles, is a journey of self-discovery and embracing a holistic approach to health and wellness. Before embarking on this transformative path, assessing your current lifestyle and health is vital. This assessment will serve as the foundation upon which you can build your personalized herbal lifestyle, tailored to meet your unique health needs and wellness goals.

1. Reflect on Your Current Diet: Take note of your daily dietary habits. What types of foods do you consume regularly? Are they alkaline, acidic, processed, or natural? Understand how your current diet may be affecting your health. Are you experiencing any digestive issues, energy fluctuations, or other health concerns that might be diet-related?

2. Evaluate Your Physical Health: Schedule a comprehensive health check-up with a healthcare professional to understand your health status. Identify any existing medical conditions, allergies, or nutritional deficiencies that may need special attention as you transition to an herbal lifestyle.

3. Assess Your Mental and Emotional Well-being: Reflect on your mental and emotional state. How do you manage stress? What practices do you have in place to support your mental health? Consider exploring mindfulness practices such as meditation or yoga, which can complement a herbal lifestyle.

4. Examine Your Lifestyle Habits: Assess your exercise routine, sleep patterns, and other lifestyle habits. Are they conducive to good health? Identify any harmful habits such as smoking or excessive alcohol consumption that may hinder your transition to a herbal lifestyle.

5. Explore Your Understanding of Herbal Remedies: Familiarize yourself with the herbal healing principles as Dr. Sebi taught. Begin exploring alkaline herbs' range and properties, and how they can be integrated into your daily routine.

6. Set Realistic Goals: Define achievable goals for transitioning to a herbal lifestyle. *What do you hope to achieve in terms of health and wellness?* Establish a realistic timeline for your transition, allowing for gradual changes and adaptation.

7. Seek Professional Guidance: Consult with a healthcare professional knowledgeable about herbal medicine and Dr. Sebi's teachings, if possible. Ensure that your transition to a herbal lifestyle is done safely, particularly if you have existing medical conditions or are on medication.

8. Document Your Journey: Keep a journal to document your experiences, observations, and the changes you notice as you transition to an herbal lifestyle. Tracking your progress will provide valuable insights and encourage you to stay committed to your wellness journey.

As Dr. Sebi advocates, embarking on the path to an herbal lifestyle is a profound commitment to nurturing your body, mind, and spirit in harmony with nature's wisdom. By meticulously assessing your current lifestyle and health, you are laying a solid foundation for a successful transition, setting the stage for a life replete with vitality, clarity, and a deep sense of wellness aligned with the natural order.

Steps Towards Adopting a Holistic Herbal Lifestyle

Adopting a holistic herbal lifestyle, especially one in alignment with Dr. Sebi's teachings, is akin to embarking on a journey back to nature's essence. It is about embracing a life that resonates with natural rhythms and herbal wisdom. Here are steps to guide you on this enriching path towards a harmonious existence.

STEP 1. Educate Yourself: Immerse yourself in the teachings of Dr. Sebi and other holistic health practitioners. Learn about the properties and benefits of alkaline herbs, and how they can contribute to achieving an alkaline body.

STEP 2. Assess Your Dietary Habits: Evaluate your current diet and identify areas where you can incorporate more alkaline foods and herbs. Slowly transition to a plant-based, alkaline diet as recommended by Dr. Sebi, reducing intake of acidic and processed foods.

STEP 3. Embrace Herbal Healing: Integrate alkaline herbs into your daily routine, whether as teas, supplements, or natural remedies. Consult with herbalists or practitioners familiar with Dr. Sebi's herbal approach to gain insights on effectively using herbs for healing and wellness.

STEP 4. Incorporate Mindfulness Practices: Engage in mindfulness practices such as meditation, yoga, and deep breathing to support your mental and emotional well-being. Cultivate a daily routine that fosters inner peace and connection to nature.

STEP 5. Foster Physical Activity: Establish a regular exercise routine that aligns with your body's needs and capabilities. Explore natural settings for physical activity like hiking, swimming, or outdoor yoga to further connect with nature.

STEP 6. Prioritize Rest and Relaxation: Ensure adequate rest and sleep to support your body's healing and rejuvenation. Create a relaxing bedtime routine that may include herbal teas that promote relaxation and restful sleep.

STEP 7. Detoxification: Engage in detoxification practices as recommended by Dr. Sebi, such as fasting or using specific herbs to cleanse the body. Listen to your body and consult with healthcare professionals to ensure detoxification is done safely.

STEP 8. Community Engagement: Connect with communities and groups who share your interest in a holistic herbal lifestyle. Sharing experiences and learning from others can be enriching and provide valuable support on your journey.

STEP 9. Regular Health Check-ups: Schedule regular health check-ups to monitor your progress and ensure that your body is responding well to the herbal lifestyle. Work with healthcare professionals who are open to or knowledgeable about holistic and herbal approaches to wellness.

STEP 10. Celebrate Your Progress: Celebrate your milestones, no matter how small, as you transition to a holistic herbal lifestyle. Reflect on the positive changes and the lessons learned, and continue to nurture your commitment to a life of holistic wellness.

Embarking on the path towards a holistic herbal lifestyle is a transformative endeavor. It's about nurturing a symbiotic relationship with nature, where the essence of herbs becomes a conduit for healing, vitality, and an elevated consciousness. By taking thoughtful steps, you are not just adopting a lifestyle, but embracing a philosophy that reveres the natural order and seeks to live in harmony with it, fostering a profound sense of well-being and a deeper connection   to   the   world   around   you.

Overcoming Common Challenges in Transition

Life is a journey of constant transition, and striving towards healing and betterment often encompasses an array of challenges. With the guidance of Dr. Sebi's teachings, adhering to an alkaline-based diet and utilizing natural herbal remedies, one can successfully navigate these hurdles in their path towards optimal health. Below are the common challenges faced during this transformative phase and provide practical solutions to overcome them.

1. The Challenge of Conflicting Information: Today's world exposes us to incredible amounts of information on health and wellness. However, not all information is accurate or beneficial. Different sources often provide conflicting views, fueling skepticism and confusion in our pursuit of wellness.

Overcoming the challenge: Dr. Sebi emphasized the importance of educating oneself on the principles behind an alkaline lifestyle before forming a personal opinion. Instead of relying solely on hearsay or media-driven narratives, invest time in reading scientific research, attending lectures or webinars from experts in the field, and actively engaging with like-minded individuals.

2. Maintaining Discipline: An alkaline-based diet requires discipline and commitment to attain desired results. Temptations can arise while dining out or celebrating holidays or gatherings where unhealthy food options are abundant.

Overcoming the challenge: Creating healthy routines is essential for success in maintaining an alkaline lifestyle. Establish clear goals, develop a meal plan designed to accommodate your week's activities, prepare meals in advance to reduce the temptation of unhealthy alternatives, and plan your grocery list strategically to eliminate processed or harmful ingredients from your kitchen.

3. Coping with Social Pressure: Those unfamiliar with Dr. Sebi's teachings may not understand the underlying principles driving your dietary choices and may pressure you into consuming harmful foods. For example, friends might insist that "just one dessert won't hurt."

Overcoming the challenge: Educate those around you about your journey by sharing the benefits of an alkaline-based lifestyle. Stress the importance of this commitment and request their understanding and support. Set boundaries; stand firm in your decision, and remind yourself of your goals.

4. Managing Stress: Stress is inevitable in life, but it can hinder the transformative process. Chronic stress can lead to unbalanced hormones, poor sleep quality, and weakened immune system, counteracting the positive impact of your lifestyle changes.

Overcoming the challenge: Develop healthy stress management techniques such as regular exercise, practicing mindfulness through meditation, yoga or journaling, and ensuring adequate rest. Incorporate Dr. Sebi's recommended herbs for stress relief, such as blue vervain or damiana, into your daily regimen.

5. Financial Considerations: Transitioning to an alkaline-based diet involves purchasing organic fruits and vegetables, often at a higher cost than conventional produce. Additionally, purchasing Dr. Sebi's herbal products may pose a financial constraint for some individuals.

Overcoming the challenge: While organic produce is ideal, if it is not financially feasible, prioritize purchasing conventional fruits and vegetables that are either in season or lower in pesticide residues. Determine which herbal remedies are most essential to your needs and invest accordingly.

6. Dealing with Detoxification Symptoms: During the initial phase of adopting an alkaline diet and incorporating herbal remedies recommended by Dr. Sebi, you may experience detoxification symptoms such as fatigue, headaches or digestive changes.

Overcoming the challenge: Be prepared for these detoxification symptoms by understanding that they are a normal part of your body's healing process. Increase water intake and consider incorporating gentle detoxifying teas like burdock root or sarsaparilla in small quantities under the supervision of a healthcare professional or holistic practitioner familiar with Dr. Sebi's framework.

By addressing these common challenges head-on and embracing a holistic approach to wellness inspired by Dr. Sebi's teachings on natural healing through nutrition and herbs, individuals can successfully overcome obstacles on their path to a revitalized life. The key lies within the cultivation of discipline, self-awareness, and unwavering commitment while continually seeking guidance from trustworthy sources.

BOOK 2: PRACTICAL APPLICATIONS OF HERBAL WELLNESS

CHAPTER 1

DAILY ROUTINES FOR LIFELONG WELLNESS

Morning Routines: Herbal Teas and Natural Detox

The sun slowly rises, as warm hues of pink, gold, and orange paint the morning sky. A new day has arrived, and it's time to nourish our bodies, minds, and spirits. Our morning rituals play a vital role in setting the tone for the day ahead.

The Power of Herbal Teas

Herbal teas are not only relaxing but also brimming with benefits for the body. They have been used for thousands of years in various cultures around the world for their medicinal properties. Dr. Sebi believed that many ailments could be prevented or even cured by consuming nature's gifts, such as herbal teas.

Packed with antioxidants, vitamins, and minerals, herbal teas have immune-boosting properties that help us maintain optimal health. By starting your day with a cup of herbal tea, you're stepping on the path to holistic living and practicing one of Dr. Sebi's principles electric foods that "feed" the body at a cellular level.

Morning routines are an essential part of our well-being. They give us an opportunity to cleanse our systems both physically and emotionally. Mindful practices such as yoga, meditation, and journaling can help set a positive tone for your day.

These rituals also offer an excellent time to incorporate herbal teas into your morning routine. As you sip on your warm beverage, focus on your intentions for the day ahead – be it personal growth, professional success or simply connecting with loved ones.

Top Herbal Teas for Morning Routines

Sarsaparilla Tea: Rich in antioxidants and known to promote liver detoxification by binding toxins that are then excreted through the kidneys. This herbal tea is excellent for kickstarting your morning detox regimen.

Ingredients:

- One tbsp dried sarsaparilla root
- Two cups boiling water

Instructions:

1. Place the dried sarsaparilla root in your teapot.
2. Pour the boiling water over your roots, then let them steep within ten mins, preferably longer.
3. Strain the tea into cups and enjoy daily for detoxification.

Stinging Nettle Tea: An anti-inflammatory powerhouse effective in easing chronic inflammation and water retention. Nettle tea is a perfect morning beverage for promoting balanced energy throughout the day.

Ingredients:

- One tbsp dried stinging nettle leaves
- Two cups boiling water

Instructions:

1. Place the dried stinging nettle leaves in your teapot.
2. Pour the boiling water over your leaves, then let them steep within five to ten mins.
3. Strain the tea into cups, then enjoy daily for balanced energy and reduced inflammation.

Red Raspberry Leaf Tea: Famed for its ability to balance hormones, this herbal tea can help alleviate mood swings and promote mental clarity. Enjoying red raspberry leaf tea in the morning can set you up for a day filled with positivity and focus.

Ingredients:

- One tbsp dried red raspberry leaves
- Two cups boiling water

Instructions:

1. Place the dried red raspberry leaves in your teapot.
2. Pour boiling water over your leaves, then let them steep within five to ten mins..
3. Strain the tea into cups, then enjoy daily for improved mental clarity and hormonal balance.

Dr. Sebi believed that our bodies are designed to self-regulate and self-heal when provided with the right conditions. He encouraged practices that embrace the body's natural ability to cleanse itself of toxins and create an environment where optimal wellness can thrive.

In addition to consuming herbal teas, start your day with alkaline water infused with lemon or lime juice on an empty stomach. This ritual helps with digestion while flushing toxins from the liver, kidneys, and skin. Dr. Sebi recommended following a plant-based alkaline diet as another powerful way to detoxify your body naturally.

Practicing deep breathing exercises in the morning not only calms your mind but also boosts oxygen levels, helping your body eliminate waste products more effectively. Engaging in activities that stimulate lymphatic drainage, such as brisk walking or rebounding, further supports detoxification. By harmonizing our body's internal processes and incorporating herbal teas into our daily rituals, we can experience improved health, enhanced well-being, and a deeper connection to our true selves.

Mid-day Routines: Managing Stress and Energy Levels

The sun is high in the sky as midday approaches, casting its warm embrace upon the earth. We find ourselves in the midst of daily responsibilities, yet it's crucial to protect our energy and establish a relationship with Mother Nature to manage stress effectively. In this section, we will explore several mid-day routines inspired by Dr. Sebi's teachings that harmonize with nature, rejuvenate our energy levels, and relieve stress.

1. Healing Nature Walks: One remarkable way to alleviate stress while replenishing energy is by taking mindful walks amidst the soothing embrace of nature. Studies have revealed that surrounding ourselves with greenery balances our mood and fosters feelings of tranquility. Immerse yourself in the world of plants by visiting a nearby forest or preserve, releasing your worries as you envelop yourself in their calming presence.

2. Mindful Breathing Exercises: Dr. Sebi advocated for conscious breathing to maintain a centered state of mind despite external stressors. The simple act of focusing on your breath can do wonders for your mental health, providing a much-needed respite from tension. Close your eyes for a moment amidst your routine and breathe deeply, inhaling through your nose and exhaling audibly through your mouth. Match equal lengths for inhalation and exhalation while focusing on each breath to clear away chattering thoughts and enhance energy flow.

3. Nourishment through Herbal Infusions: As part of Dr. Sebi's philosophy, herbal infusion plays an essential role in neutralizing toxins while fostering vitality. Incorporating natural herbs during the midday between meals delivers soothing relief from stress and ensures sustained replenishment of vital nutrients.

Chamomile infusion soothes persistent pressure while promoting relaxation with subtle floral notes dancing on your palate. To invigorate the senses and revive depleted energy levels, experiment with energizing herbs such as wild sarsaparilla or damiana.

4. Nap and Visualization: Sometimes, we may experience an energy slump during midday, which can be alleviated by taking a short, revitalizing nap. This pause is crucial to restore mental clarity and release accumulated stress. During your nap, visualize yourself surrounded by vibrant, flourishing greenery growing robust, resilient roots beneath your feet. This mental imagery provides additional sustenance, expanding your sense of connection with nature and grounding you in the present moment.

5. Midday Movement: Ever feel the stress accumulate within your muscles till it's almost unbearable? The solution might be closer than you think – our bodies crave movement to allay the tension coiling inside us. Simple exercises such as stretching your limbs or gentle yoga can offer profound relief while helping you recharge from within.

6. Herbal Baths for Relaxation and Rejuvenation: Drawing on Dr. Sebi's healing practices, herbal baths act as powerful remedies for regenerating one's inner strength and cleansing the body of toxins. Mid-day offers an ideal opportunity to indulge in a therapeutic soak infused with revitalizing herbs to unite body, mind, and spirit harmoniously. Consider using herbs such as lavender or sage to create a calm atmosphere that permeates your senses with tranquility.

7. Connecting with the Earth: Lastly, one of Dr. Sebi's core teachings emphasizes the importance of connecting with Mother Earth, both physically and spiritually. The world holds infinite wisdom waiting to be unearthed by those who seek it. Allocate time during the mid-day to sit barefoot on grass or soil, imagining a deep-rooted connection between you and the earth, drawing sustenance from her nurturing embrace.

Make kindness towards yourself a priority amidst the flurry of everyday challenges by embracing nature-inspired midday routines. Listen to Dr. Sebi's wisdom on nurturing our physical bodies through herbal infusions while caring for our mental wellbeing through conscious breathing and visualization exercises. By doing so, you will invite stability and vitality to flourish, guiding your journey towards holistic wellness.

Evening Routines: Promoting Restful Sleep and Rejuvenation

It is essential to establish healthy evening routines that will help us unwind from the day, alleviate stress, and prepare our bodies and minds for a peaceful night of restorative sleep. An effective evening routine helps our body transition from the hectic activities of the day to a state of relaxation and tranquility. By indulging in calming rituals before bedtime, we can significantly improve the quality of our sleep, recharge our energy levels, and enhance our physical and mental well-being.

Dr. Sebi believed in harnessing the power of nature to promote restful sleep and rejuvenation. Below are essential components of an evening routine based on his teachings:

1. Engage in gentle physical activity: Dr. Sebi emphasized the importance of staying physically active throughout the day. In the evening, opt for light exercises, such as stretching, yoga, or tai chi, to help release tension from your body and gain mental clarity.

2. Soothe your senses with calming scents: Aromatherapy has been widely recognized for its ability to reduce anxiety and improve sleep quality. Incorporate essential oils like lavender, chamomile, or bergamot into your evening rituals. Apart from diffusers or candles, you can also add a few drops to your pillowcase or bathwater for an immersive experience.

3. Optimize your bedroom environment: Adjusting the ambiance in your sleeping quarters is crucial for optimal rest and rejuvenation. Keep electronic devices away from your bedside table; maintain a clutter-free space; invest in comfortable bedding; and regulate room temperature to around 60-67°F.

4. Promote relaxation through herbal teas: Dr. Sebi recommended sipping on herbal teas as part of your pre-bedtime routine. Some of his favorites included chamomile, lemon balm, and passionflower, which are known for their calming properties.

5. Nurture emotional well-being: Set aside 10-15 mins each evening to process your thoughts and emotions constructively. Journaling, meditation, deep breathing exercises, or engaging in spiritual practices can elevate your mood and prepare you for a restful night's sleep.

6. Embrace sleep-supporting bedtime habits: Abstain from caffeine and alcohol consumption close to bedtime; avoid heavy meals; and minimize screen time at least one hour before sleep.

Dr. Sebi's Herbs for Sleep and Rejuvenation

Dr. Sebi strongly advocated the use of herbs to enhance the quality of our sleep and rejuvenation process. Below are some powerful herbs mentioned in his teachings that can be incorporated into our evening routines:

1. Valerian Root: This herb is widely recognized for its ability to reduce anxiety and induce a peaceful night's sleep. It's available in various forms, such as capsules, teas, tinctures, or liquid extracts.

2. Passionflower: An effective remedy for promoting calmness and reducing anxiety levels, passionflower can be consumed as a tea infusion or taken in capsule form.

3. St. John's Wort: This herb has a remarkable impact on our mental well-being by acting as a natural anti-depressant and promoting emotional stability — essential for those struggling with insomnia caused by stress or anxiety.

4. Lemon Balm (Melissa officinalis): Lemon balm elicits a soothing effect on the mind and body, making it an ideal addition to your evening routine.

Investing time in creating a personalized evening routine based on Dr. Sebi's herbal bible can be highly rewarding as it contributes to a restful sleep, improved mental clarity, and a harmonious relationship between the mind, body, and spirit.

CHAPTER 2

HERBAL REMEDIES FOR COMMON AILMENTS

Herbal Treatments for Digestive Issues, Headaches, and Skin Problems

In our modern society, we are increasingly exposed to dietary and environmental factors that take a toll on our digestive health, mental wellbeing, and skin conditions. Thankfully, the wisdom of Dr. Sebi's herbal teachings offer holistic and natural solutions to these common ailments. In this chapter, we will cover various herbal treatments for digestive issues, headaches, and skin problems.

Herbal Treatments for Digestive Issues

Digestive issues can cause discomfort that affects our everyday lives. Dr. Sebi's herbal remedies provide an all-natural way to address these concerns without causing additional harm to the body.

Burdock Root: One of the most helpful herbs for digestive issues is burdock root. It aids in detoxifying the body by removing toxins from the blood, which ultimately improves digestion. It also possesses anti-inflammatory properties that alleviate gastrointestinal distress. To make *burdock root tea*, you will need:

- Two tbsp dried burdock root
- Four cups water
- Sweetener of choice (optional)

Instructions:

1. Let water boil in your saucepan. Add the dried burdock root, then adjust to a simmer within twenty mins till liquid has reduced by half.
2. Remove, then strain the tea into your teapot. Sweeten using your preferred sweetener (optional). Drink this tea daily for optimal digestive benefits.

Fennel: This aromatic herb soothes digestion by reducing abdominal cramps and gas production. Its mild diuretic effects help expel excess fluid from the body and prevent bloating. To make *fennel seed tea*, you will need:

- One tbsp fennel seeds, crushed
- Two cups water
- Honey or sweetener of choice (optional)

Instructions:

1. Boil water in your saucepan. Add crushed fennel seeds, then adjust to a simmer. Let it steep within ten mins till desired strength is reached.
2. Strain the tea into your teapot, then sweeten with honey or preferred sweetener if desired. Drink this tea warm, twice daily, preferably after meals.

Ginger: A powerful anti-inflammatory agent, ginger improves digestion by stimulating digestive juices and enzymes. As an added bonus, it also provides relief from nausea or vomiting associated with various gastrointestinal conditions. To make *ginger tea*, you will need:

- One tbsp grated ginger root, fresh
- Two cups water
- Honey or sweetener of choice (optional)
- Lemon juice (optional)

Instructions:

1. Boil water in your saucepan. Add the grated ginger, then adjust to a simmer within ten mins till liquid has reduced by half.
2. Strain the tea into your teapot, then sweeten with honey or preferred sweetener if desired.
3. Add desired amount of honey or sweetener (optional) and lemon juice (optional) for additional flavor and benefits. Serve.

Herbal Treatments for Headaches

Headaches can be debilitating and hinder productivity; luckily, Dr. Sebi's herbal treatments offer gentle relief without resorting to over-the-counter medications that may have side effects.

Feverfew: This herb boasts anti-inflammatory properties that make it highly effective in treating headaches. It helps alleviate pain and inflammation by hindering the release of prostaglandins—a compound known to cause swelling in blood vessels. To make *feverfew tea*, you will need:

- One tsp dried feverfew leaves
- One cup boiling water

Instructions:

1. Place the dried feverfew leaves in your teapot. Pour the boiling water, then let it steep within fifteen mins.
2. Strain your tea, then drink one cup feverfew tea right after you start experiencing headache symptoms. You can also consume the tea as a preventative measure by drinking one cup daily.

Peppermint: A popular remedy for headaches, peppermint contains menthol which has a cooling effect on tight muscles surrounding the skull. It's also known to soothe spasms and decrease pain perception. To make *Peppermint Tension Relief Oil*, you will need:

- Ten drops of peppermint essential oil
- Two tbsp carrier oil (e.g., sweet almond oil or coconut oil)

Instructions:

1. Mix peppermint essential oil plus your chosen carrier oil in your small container. Seal tightly, then shake well till blended.
2. Apply a small amount of your peppermint tension relief oil to your temples, the back of your neck, and your wrists. Gently massage the oil into your skin, and reapply as needed throughout the day.

Skullcap: This potent herb is known to fight headaches by relieving tension and anxiety. Additionally, it promotes relaxation and rejuvenation of the nervous system. To make *Skullcap Relaxation Tincture*, you will need:

- Quarter cup dried skullcap
- One cup vodka or other high-proof alcohol

Instructions:

1. Put dried skullcap in your clean glass jar. Pour the alcohol, cover, then store it in your cool, dark place within four weeks.

2. Shake your jar gently every few days to help extract the active compounds from the skullcap.

3. After four weeks, strain the liquid through, discarding the solid plant material. Store the tincture in your amber glass dropper bottle.

4. Take twenty to thirty drops of skullcap relaxation tincture every six hours as needed for headache relief.

Herbal Treatments for Skin Problems

With an increase in environmental toxins and pollutants, skin problems have become prevalent. Dr. Sebi's teachings provide a range of herbs that promote healthy skin while addressing other internal issues that contribute to skin concerns.

Dandelion: Rich in antioxidants, dandelion helps protect the skin by neutralizing free radicals responsible for cellular damage. Its detoxifying properties help cleanse the liver, which plays a crucial role in promoting healthy, glowing skin. To make a *Dandelion Tea*, you will need:

- Two cups fresh dandelion leaves, chopped roughly
- Four cups water
- Honey (optional)

Instructions:

1. Boil the water in your pot. Add the chopped leaves, then let it steep within ten mins.

2. Strain the mixture into your cup. Add honey if desired. Drink one to two cups dandelion tea daily to support healthy skin.

Mullein: This herb is known for its emollient properties that soothe skin inflammations, such as eczema or psoriasis. Additionally, mullein assists in cell rejuvenation by improving blood circulation. To make a *Mullein Oil Remedy*, you will need:

- One cup dried mullein flowers
- Two cups olive oil

Instructions:

1. Place dried mullein flowers in your glass jar. Pour olive oil over your flowers till they are fully submerged.

2. Cover, then it in a sunny spot within four weeks. After this period, strain your oil using cheesecloth into another jar.

3. Apply mullein oil directly to affected areas once or twice daily for soothing relief from inflammation or irritation.

Sarsaparilla: Renowned for its tonic and blood-purifying abilities, sarsaparilla supports immune function while promoting healthy skin by cleansing toxins from the body. To make a *Sarsaparilla Tea,* you will need:

- One tbsp dried sarsaparilla root
- Four cups of water
- Honey (optional)

Instructions:

1. Let water boil in your pot. Add dried sarsaparilla root, then let it simmer within twenty mins.
2. Strain your tea and add honey if desired. Drink one cup of sarsaparilla tea daily for optimal skin health benefits.

Dr. Sebi's herbal treatments offer an array of natural remedies for ailments such as digestive issues, headaches, and skin problems. They not only address immediate concerns but also work on increasing overall health and well-being by eliminating toxins from the body and strengthening the immune system. By incorporating these herbs into your daily regime, you can harness their healing powers to revitalize your physical and emotional well-being without relying on artificial or chemical-laden treatments. It is imperative to consult with a knowledgeable health practitioner before incorporating these herbs into your routine to ensure their suitability for your specific needs. Remember that each individual's constitution varies, and what works best for one may not work equally well for another person. Take the time to research further on these natural remedies and consider including them in your diet according to Dr. Sebi's alkaline dietary recommendations. Let the power of herbs work its wonders on your digestive health, headaches, and skin conditions so that you may lead a healthier, more radiant life in harmony with nature.

Addressing Emotional Wellness: Anxiety, Stress, and Depression

Emotional wellness is an essential aspect of a person's overall health. Addressing mental health issues like anxiety, stress, and depression has been a long-standing challenge for people worldwide. Conventional therapies often involve medication and therapy. However, in the Dr. Sebi herbal healing philosophy, natural remedies are the preferred path towards emotional well-being.

Emotional wellness refers to an individual's mental state and their ability to maintain a semblance of balance amidst life's challenges. It is crucial that one's emotional well-being is maintained and nurtured because it highly affects other areas of life such as physical health, relationships, work performance, and overall quality of life.

Anxiety, stress, and depression are common mental health issues that can affect anyone regardless of age or demographic origin. These conditions demand attention as they can potentially lead to more severe health complications if left untreated.

Herbal Remedies vs Conventional Medication

In recent years, natural remedies such as herbal therapies have gained popularity over conventional treatment methods due to their reduced side effects and their compatibility with holistic perspectives on well-being.

Herbal treatments provide essential nutrients required by the human body while eliminating processed chemicals present in most medicines. This practice aligns with Dr. Sebi's central doctrine about the Alkaline diet's role in maintaining physical and mental harmony.

The Role of the Alkaline Diet in Emotional Wellness

A pivotal aspect of Dr. Sebi's teachings was centered around the consumption of alkaline foods while avoiding acidic substances that can cause harm to our bodies. This philosophy extends to emotional wellness and the use of alkaline herbs to treat anxiety, stress, and depression.

An often-ignored contributor to emotional instability is diet. The food we consume can directly impact our mental state, as certain foods can cause chemical imbalances within our bodies resulting in emotional instability. A diet that is rich in alkaline foods aids in cleansing the body and maintaining balance internally.

Utilizing Herbs for Emotional Wellness

Dr. Sebi's extensive knowledge of herbs allows us to dive into their psychological benefits when addressing mental health issues such as anxiety, stress, and depression. Below, we discuss some basic principles when using herbs for emotional well-being:

1. Balanced approach: It is vital to adopt a holistic approach when incorporating herbal remedies for emotional wellness. One must strive to maintain a balanced lifestyle by incorporating fresh fruits, vegetables, as well as exercise to ensure harmony between body and mind.

2. Gradual introduction: Introduce herbs to your daily routine gradually while allowing your body sufficient time to adjust. Observe any changes in emotions or mood that follow the introduction of these natural substances.

3. Be mindful: Pay attention to what you're feeling at every stage of this journey towards emotional balance. Regularly check in with yourself while utilizing these remedies to determine how they're affecting you.

4. Consult professionals: Last but not least, always consult with healthcare professionals before adding new herbs or supplements into your regimen.

Herbal Remedies for Emotional Wellness

As our hectic lifestyles take over, emotional wellness often takes a backseat. Anxiety, stress, and depression are common challenges that millions of people face every day. The good news is that there are herbal remedies that can help alleviate these emotional concerns without resorting to pharmaceutical drugs. Below are some herbal remedies that your body will appreciate, according to the teachings of Dr. Sebi.

Calming Infusion Tea

Ingredients:

- One part passionflower (fresh or dried)
- One part lemon balm (fresh or dried)
- One part chamomile flowers (dried)
- Eight oz water
- One tbsp raw agave nectar or maple syrup (optional)

Instructions:

1. Mix equal parts of passionflower, lemon balm, and chamomile flowers in your jar. Boil water in your pot.
2. Place one tbsp herbal mixture into your teacup. Pour the boiling water over your herbs, cover, then let it steep within ten mins.
3. Strain it into your cup. Sweeten with raw agave nectar or maple syrup as desired.

4. Drink one cup of this calming infusion two times a day, preferably in the morning and in the evening before bedtime, to help combat anxiety and stress.

Mood Uplifting Tincture

Ingredients:

- Four oz dried St. John's Wort
- Sixteen oz vegetable glycerin

Instructions:

1. Fill your glass jar with the dried St. John's Wort, leaving one-inch head space. Slowly pour vegetable glycerin into your jar.
2. Mix well using your wooden spoon, removing air bubbles. Seal your jar tightly with its lid. Label it with the date and ingredients used.
3. Store the tincture in your cool, dark place within four to six weeks, giving it a good shake every few days.
4. After four to six weeks of steeping, strain the herbs out of the glycerin using your fine mesh strainer.
5. Store your mood-uplifting tincture in an amber glass dropper bottle for easy use. Administer 20 to 30 drops under your tongue or mixed in water, up to three times per day.

Nervine Herbal Bath

Ingredients:

- Half cup dried lavender flowers
- Half cup dried chamomile flowers
- Half cup dried rose petals

Instructions:

1. Mix all dried herbs in your container. Place the herbal mixture into your muslin drawstring bag.
2. Securely close the bag or cheesecloth so that none of the herbs can escape.
3. Run a warm bath and add your herb-filled muslin bag or cheesecloth directly into the water while it runs.
4. in this relaxation-inducing herbal bath within twenty to thirty mins, allowing yourself to unwind and find relief from stress and anxiety.

It is important to note that while these herbal remedies may provide relief from anxiety, stress, and depression, they are not meant as replacements for professional medical advice. If you have severe mental health issues or are currently taking medication for your emotional well-being, ensure that you consult a healthcare professional before using these remedies. Each person's body and experience with herbs might be different, so experiment cautiously and choose the herbal treatment that best suits your individual needs.

By incorporating these natural remedies into our daily routine, we can demonstrate our commitment to living a balanced life and improving our emotional well-being. When we prioritize emotional wellness, we prioritize ourselves and give our minds the tools they need to flourish. With the proper herbal support, we have the power to overcome stress and anxiety, allowing us to live harmoniously with ourselves and the world around us.

Building a Basic Herbal First-Aid Kit

An herbal first-aid kit offers natural solutions for addressing common health issues such as colds, minor cuts, and insect bites. When paired with conventional medicine, such kits can provide well-rounded care for various health concerns. Its advantages include improved overall wellbeing, reduced side effects, and self-reliance during emergencies. Here are some essential items to include in your Dr. Sebi-inspired herbal first-aid kit:

1. Irish Sea Moss (Chondrus crispus): Known for its ability to nourish the skin and support respiratory health, Irish sea moss contains minerals like zinc, iodine, iron, and calcium. It helps reduce inflammation and can be utilized as an expectorant to break up mucus in the body.

2. Bladderwrack (Fucus vesiculosus): Bladderwrack supports thyroid function by providing iodine, an essential element needed for the production of thyroid hormones. It is beneficial in treating conditions such as thyroid dysfunction, obesity, arthritis, and digestive ailments.

3. Elderberry (Sambucus nigra): Elderberry is acclaimed for its antiviral properties, helping combat colds and flu symptoms by boosting the immune system. Consume it as a syrup or prepare it as a tea to enjoy its therapeutic benefits.

4. Nettle Leaf (Urtica dioica): Nettle is a potent anti-inflammatory herb that assists in relieving joint pain and muscle spasms. Furthermore, it aids in detoxifying the body by purging toxins from the blood.

5. Sarsaparilla (Smilax ornata): Sarsaparilla is a prominent herb in Dr. Sebi's teachings, known for its cooling and purifying properties. It can alleviate skin conditions like eczema, psoriasis, and dermatitis by cleansing the blood and lymphatic system.

6. Yellow Dock (Rumex crispus): Yellow dock is useful for detoxification, as it works as a gentle laxative to expel toxins through the digestive tract. It also aids in restoring equilibrium to the body by helping with iron absorption, making it beneficial for individuals suffering from anemia.

7. Burdock Root (Arctium lappa): Burdock root is a powerful diuretic and detoxifier that helps support liver function. Additionally, it has anti-inflammatory properties and aids in maintaining balanced blood sugar levels.

8. Mullein Leaf (Verbascum thapsus): Mullein is valuable in treating respiratory issues such as asthma, coughs, and bronchitis, due to its expectorant and anti-inflammatory characteristics. Prepare it as a tea or consume in capsule form.

9. Plantain Leaf (Plantago major): Plantain leaf acts as an antibacterial and has astringent properties that make it an excellent remedy for minor cuts and bug bites.

10. Cayenne Pepper (Capsicum annuum): Cayenne pepper is helpful in treating minor digestive problems like gas and indigestion while also increasing circulation throughout the body.

11. Slippery Elm Bark (Ulmus rubra): Slippery elm helps alleviate digestive issues such as heartburn and irritable bowel syndrome by forming a protective layer on mucous membranes.

12. Valerian Root (Valeriana officinalis): Valerian root aids in calming nerves, reducing anxiety, and promoting sleep due to its sedative effects.

Store your herbal first-aid kit in a cool, dry place away from direct sunlight and moisture. Ensure that all herbs, tinctures, and salves are properly labeled with their names, expiration dates, and dosage guidelines.

Building a Dr. Sebi-inspired herbal first-aid kit allows you to harness the healing power of Mother Nature for overall wellbeing. Keep in mind that it is crucial to consult with a healthcare professional before incorporating any herbs into your routine or treating specific conditions. By assembling a basic herbal first-aid kit based on Dr. Sebi's teachings, you'll have natural remedies at your disposal to help manage minor health concerns and improve your quality of life.

CHAPTER 3

HERBAL WELLNESS FOR CHRONIC CONDITIONS

Herbal Support for Conditions Like Diabetes, Arthritis and High Blood Pressure

Living with chronic health conditions, such as diabetes, arthritis, and high blood pressure can be challenging and overwhelming. Conventional treatments often come with various side effects and, in some cases, may be out of reach due to financial constraints. Dr. Sebi's Herbal Bible provides alternative solutions to these challenges by offering herbal support for people living with such health conditions.

Herbal remedies have played a significant role in traditional medicine for thousands of years. Today, they still offer countless benefits for those seeking natural alternatives to support their well-being. This section explores the herbal remedies that Dr. Sebi formulated to aid individuals suffering from these conditions.

1. Diabetes: Diabetes is a metabolic disorder characterized by elevated blood sugar (glucose) levels resulting from issues with insulin production or its effectiveness within the body. The two primary types of diabetes are type 1 (insulin-dependent) and type 2 (non-insulin-dependent). Dr. Sebi's herbal remedies for diabetes primarily focus on maintaining healthy blood sugar levels and supporting the pancreas in producing insulin. Some of his recommended herbs include:

1. Cinnamon: Known for its ability to lower blood glucose levels, cinnamon is a popular choice in managing type 2 diabetes. Consuming this spice regularly can help improve insulin sensitivity and slow down carbohydrate digestion while reducing fasting glucose levels.

2. Gymnema Sylvestre: Also referred to as 'gurmar' or 'sugar destroyer,' Gymnema sylvestre is an Ayurvedic herb that supports pancreas function and reduces sugar cravings. It works by stimulating insulin secretion and lowering blood sugar concentrations.

3. Fenugreek: Studies have shown that fenugreek consumption can lead to improved glucose tolerance and reduced blood sugar levels. The herb contains amino acids that

52

stimulate insulin production in the body, and its fiber content slows carbohydrate absorption, effectively maintaining stable glucose levels.

2. Arthritis: Arthritis is an umbrella term that encompasses over 100 different inflammatory joint diseases. The two most common types are osteoarthritis, which results from wear and tear of the joints, and rheumatoid arthritis, an autoimmune disease causing inflammation in the joints. Dr. Sebi's herbal remedies for arthritis aim to reduce inflammation, alleviate pain, and promote joint health. Recommended herbs include:

1. Turmeric: Containing a potent anti-inflammatory compound called curcumin, turmeric has long been used in treating arthritis symptoms. Regular intake can help reduce inflammation and pain associated with joint conditions.

2. Ginger: With its powerful antioxidant properties, ginger helps fight inflammation in arthritic joints and offers pain relief. Incorporating ginger into your diet or consuming it as an herbal supplement can benefit those with arthritis.

3. Stinging Nettle: Known for its anti-inflammatory properties, stinging nettle can help manage arthritis by reducing pain and inflammation in the joints. Drinking nettle leaf tea or using topically as an oil is beneficial for individuals suffering from arthritis.

3. High Blood Pressure: High blood pressure often results from multiple factors including stress, age, diet, or genetics affecting proper blood circulation. In many cases, lifestyle changes can bring improvement; however, sometimes additional support is needed to maintain healthy blood pressure levels. Dr. Sebi's herbal recommendations for high blood pressure include:

1. Garlic: This powerful herb contains allicin, which has been shown to reduce blood pressure by promoting vasodilation of blood vessels. Consuming garlic regularly can help lower high blood pressure over time.

2. Hawthorn: Used traditionally for heart-related ailments, hawthorn is rich in antioxidants that help dilate blood vessels and improve blood flow. Regular consumption of this herb can significantly lower high blood pressure.

3. Hibiscus: Drinking hibiscus tea regularly can provide an excellent source of antioxidants and help lower blood pressure. It acts as a natural diuretic, removing excess sodium from the body and reducing pressure on blood vessel walls.

While herbal remedies can offer incredible support for managing chronic health conditions, it is crucial to consult a healthcare professional before incorporating these herbs into your daily routine. Combining the wisdom of Dr. Sebi's Herbal Bible with professional guidance ensures a personalized, holistic approach to improving your health and well-being.

A Look at Dr. Sebi's Approach to More Severe Diseases

Dr. Sebi's herbal treatments have been widely praised for their unique methods and positive impacts on people's lives. Throughout his career, he had worked on several severe diseases and proposed alternative, natural ways to combat them. In this section, we will delve deeper into Dr. Sebi's approach to some more severe diseases, drawing from his expertise and dedication to natural remedies.

1. Cancer: One of the most widespread and feared diseases globally, cancer has many types and can affect almost any part of the body. Traditional medicine offers various treatments such as surgery, chemoand radiation therapy; however, these can cause numerous side effects that might weaken a patient even further.

In contrast, Dr. Sebi took a different path in dealing with cancer patients. His approach relies on purifying the body by eradicating mucus and stimulating cell regeneration. According to him, mucus is the root cause of all diseases – including cancer – because it creates an ideal environment for harmful cells to thrive.

To eliminate mucus from the body, Dr. Sebi prescribed certain herbs like Burdock Root (Arctium lappa), Nettle (Urtica dioica), and Yellow Dock (Rumex crispus). These plants work together to cleanse the bloodstream and help boost the immune system. Dr. Sebi also emphasized consuming alkaline foods from his unique nutritional guide, such as fresh fruits, vegetables, nuts, and seeds. This diet helps restore balance within the body and provides essential nutrients to improve overall health.

2. Alzheimer's Disease: Characterized by progressive cognitive decline that affects memory and thinking skills, Alzheimer's disease is another severe ailment that lacks a cure in conventional medicine. Nonetheless, Dr. Sebi was confident that through dietary changes and specific herbal medicines, one could manage this degenerative condition.

Dr. Sebi's approach to Alzheimer's disease focused on eliminating mucus and heavy metals from the body, which he believed could aggravate the condition. By doing so, he aimed to improve brain function and restore proper communication between cells.

Some of the essential herbs recommended by Dr. Sebi for Alzheimer's patients include Gingko Biloba (Ginkgo biloba) and St. John's Wort (Hypericum perforatum). These herbs work together to enhance cognitive abilities while providing overall relaxation and stress relief to the patient.

In addition to herbal remedies, Dr. Sebi's alkaline diet played a vital role in managing Alzheimer's symptoms. He advised consuming natural, minimally processed foods that contain high amounts of antioxidants, vitamins, and minerals. This dietary plan would help protect and nourish brain cells, as well as reduce inflammation within the body.

3. AIDS/HIV: Dr. Sebi was well-known for his controversial claim that he could cure AIDS using natural remedies. Although these claims were met with skepticism from the mainstream medical community, Dr. Sebi still treated and claimed that several patients were cured by following his regimen.

His approach to treating HIV/AIDS centered around strengthening the immune system so that it could effectively fight back against viral infections like HIV. Dr. Sebi believed that clearing out mucus from the body was essential in battling HIV/AIDS because it promoted improved lymphatic system function and detoxification processes.

Some of the leading herbs used by Dr. Sebi for AIDS/HIV treatment include Viento (Phytolacca spp.), Red Clover (Trifolium pratense), and Blessed Thistle (Cnicus benedictus). These plants work synergistically to cleanse the bloodstream, stimulate detoxification organs like the liver and kidneys, boost immunity, and naturally fight off infections.

While traditional medicine plays an undeniable role in treating severe diseases worldwide, Dr. Sebi's holistic approach to health care provides an interesting alternative. Centered on the belief that mucus build-up and acidity in the body leads to various ailments, Dr. Sebi's natural remedies promote disease prevention and healing through herbs and an alkaline diet.

Though conventional medicine may view Dr. Sebi's claims with skepticism, many of his teachings continue to resonate with people seeking alternative methods for better health. Although this chapter focused on severe conditions like cancer, Alzheimer's disease, and HIV/AIDS, it is essential to consult with your healthcare professional before making any treatments or dietary changes.

Working With Healthcare Providers For A Holistic Treatment Plan

When developing a holistic treatment plan, it's essential to involve healthcare providers experienced in both conventional medicine and natural therapies. These professionals have the knowledge and expertise to guide you through the process of combining the best of both worlds – modern medicine and traditional herbal remedies.

Collaborating with a diverse team of healthcare providers can provide valuable insights and advice on how to achieve optimal health through a balanced and comprehensive treatment plan. Some of the professionals you may consider including in your team are:

- Primary care physicians
- Naturopathic doctors
- Registered dietitians or nutritionists
- Clinical herbalists
- Acupuncturists
- Massage therapists
- Chiropractors

Communicating Your Health Goals and Needs

To create a successful holistic treatment plan, open communication is essential between you and your healthcare team. Begin by sharing your health goals and any specific concerns that you have related to the implementation of Dr. Sebi's Herbal Bible principles. It's also vital to discuss any pre-existing medical conditions, medications, or treatments you are currently using to ensure that integrating herbal remedies into your care will not pose any risks or interfere with existing treatments. Make sure to ask questions about dietary changes, exercise programs, stress management techniques, or other lifestyle adjustments that can enhance your overall well-being in addition to using Dr. Sebi-approved herbs.

Developing an Individualized Treatment Plan

A well-designed holistic treatment plan will take into account your unique health situation and needs. Keep in mind that a one-size-fits-all approach does not exist, and your healthcare providers must work together to ensure that the strategies used are tailored to your requirements.

Your individualized treatment plan might include:

1. Nutritional counseling and meal planning based on Dr. Sebi's nutritional guidelines
2. Identifying the appropriate herbs from Dr. Sebi's Herbal Bible to address specific health concerns
3. Developing a detoxification plan using Dr. Sebi's approved methods
4. Incorporating stress reduction techniques such as yoga, meditation, or tai chi
5. Regular exercise routine creation that complements your lifestyle

Be prepared to follow up with your healthcare team regularly, review your progress, and make any necessary adjustments.

Advocating for Yourself

As a patient seeking holistic care, it is crucial to advocate for yourself in conversations with healthcare providers. This includes ensuring that your providers understand and respect your desire to incorporate natural therapies into your treatment plan. Here are some tips on how to advocate for yourself:

1. Practice open communication: Share your concerns and remind them of your interest in incorporating Dr. Sebi's Herbal Bible principles into your care.

2. Stay informed: Educate yourself about the herbs you want to use, their potential risks and benefits, and evidence supporting their use.

3. Ask for referrals: If you feel like a provider is dismissive of your desire for a more holistic approach, seek another practitioner who is more supportive.

4. Be persistent: You have a right to pursue the treatment plan you feel is best for you; don't be afraid to stand up for yourself.

By collaborating with healthcare providers, implementing Dr. Sebi's Herbal Bible teachings, and pursuing a more comprehensive approach to wellness, you are embracing the journey towards better health. Remember that developing a holistic treatment plan is an ongoing process. It requires adaptation, patience, and understanding to create the best possible strategy for you. It is crucial to maintain a strong relationship with your healthcare team and trust one another as you work together towards improving your health and achieving the vision of holistic well-being inspired by Dr. Sebi's Herbal Bible principles.

CHAPTER 4

SUPPORTING OPTIMAL WOMEN'S HEALTH THROUGH HERBS

Balancing Hormones Naturally

In the pursuit of optimal health and well-being, women often face unique challenges due to the complex interplay of hormones. Hormonal imbalances can lead to a myriad of health issues, ranging from fatigue and mood swings to weight gain and infertility. Thankfully, there are numerous natural remedies to help balance these hormones as well as support overall wellness.

The teachings of Dr. Sebi emphasize the significance of plant-based nutrition in balancing hormones and maintaining women's health. By adopting his principles, women can find relief from common hormone-related conditions, such as premenstrual syndrome (PMS), polycystic ovary syndrome (PCOS), and menopause.

Let's explore various strategies backed by Dr. Sebi's Herbal Bible to harmonize hormones naturally.

1. Adopt a Plant-Based Diet: At the heart of Dr. Sebi's approach is the reliance on plant-based nutrition for overall well-being. Consuming a balanced diet rich in whole grains, legumes, nuts, seeds, fruits, and vegetables helps regulate hormones by providing essential nutrients for hormone synthesis and eliminating harmful toxins. A few examples of nutrient-rich foods include:

a) *Amaranth:* A gluten-free grain packed with protein and crucial minerals that support hormonal balance.

b) *Walnuts:* Rich in omega-3 fatty acids, they reduce inflammation and promote healthy hormone production.

c) *Avocado*: High in healthy fats and fiber that nourish hormone-producing glands.

d) *Sea moss:* Contains iodine which is critical for thyroid hormones.

By following Dr. Sebi's alkaline diet plan—predominantly focusing on electric foods—it becomes easier to achieve hormonal harmony while improving physical energy levels and emotional stability.

2. Herbs for Hormonal Balance: Throughout history, herbs have been used extensively in medicine with impressive abilities to restore hormonal imbalances. Dr. Sebi highlights several potent herbs, often overlooked in conventional medicine, that specifically target female hormonal issues.

a) *Chaste Tree Berry:* Also known as Vitex agnus-castus, this herb has a lengthy history of usage in treating PMS and regulating menstrual cycles. It contains active compounds that stimulate the production of luteinizing hormone, which helps balance progesterone and estrogen levels.

b) *Maca Root:* Indigenous to the Andean mountains, maca root is well-recognized for its adaptogenic properties. It stabilizes cortisol levels and fosters hormone production through nourishing the hypothalamus and pituitary glands.

c) *Black Cohosh:* Renowned for alleviating menopausal symptoms such as hot flashes and mood swings, black cohosh features phytoestrogens that mimic the body's natural estrogens, restoring balance during periods of hormonal fluctuations.

3. Stress Management: Chronic stress can impair hormonal balance by elevating cortisol levels, thus disrupting other essential hormones. To counteract this effect, practicing relaxation techniques such as deep-breathing exercises, meditation, and yoga can help regulate cortisol and restore overall hormonal harmony.

4. Exercise Regularly: Physical activity not only promotes weight control and cardiovascular health but also plays a vital role in optimizing hormone levels. Consistent exercise aids in blood sugar regulation by increasing insulin sensitivity. This factor is crucial for conditions like PCOS where insulin resistance often exacerbates hormonal imbalances.

5. Quality Sleep: Adequate sleep is indispensable for balanced hormones since it contributes to the regulation of cortisol, insulin, leptin, and ghrelin—hormones responsible for stress response and appetite. Aim for seven to eight hours of uninterrupted sleep each night to provide your body with the necessary restorative time.

6. Limit Exposure to Endocrine Disruptors: Endocrine-disrupting chemicals (EDCs) are synthetic compounds found in many everyday products such as cleaning agents, plastics, and cosmetics. They can interfere with hormone production and regulation, leading to numerous health issues. By opting for eco-friendly and natural alternatives, women can reduce their exposure to EDCs and promote hormonal equilibrium.

Balancing hormones naturally for women's health is achievable by adhering to Dr. Sebi's principles of plant-based nutrition, utilizing herbal remedies, managing stress, exercising regularly, obtaining quality sleep, and minimizing exposure to endocrine disruptors. By taking a holistic approach toward hormonal balance, women can achieve improved physical and emotional well-being while alleviating many common hormone-related health issues.

Enhancing Fertility with Herbs

For centuries, women have turned to nature's abundance of medicinal plants to promote their reproductive well-being. The famous healer Dr. Sebi recognized the potent remedies found in herbs and incorporated them into his holistic approach to healing. An essential step towards improving fertility is understanding the crucial role that a woman's overall health plays in her ability to conceive. A balanced diet, regular exercise, and proper stress-management all contribute to reproductive health by supporting hormonal balance and an optimally functioning reproductive system.

However, even with these healthy habits in place, sometimes the body needs some extra help. This is where the amazing wisdom of herbs comes into play.

1. **Red Raspberry Leaf:** Red raspberry leaf has been used by women for generations to support their reproductive health. Rich in vitamins and minerals, it aids in strengthening the uterine walls and balancing hormones. By promoting a healthy menstrual cycle and alleviating symptoms of PMS, red raspberry leaf can help prepare the body for conception.
2. **Nettle leaf:** Nettle leaf is considered a highly nourishing herb because it is packed with essential vitamins and minerals that support overall health and wellness. For women trying to conceive, nettle leaf can help purify the blood, reduce inflammation, and promote hormonal balance, thereby creating a healthy environment for fertilization.
3. **Maca Root:** This Peruvian superfood is known for its fertility-enhancing properties. Maca root works by supporting the endocrine system and regulating the production of hormones. For women who struggle with hormone imbalances or those with conditions such as PCOS, incorporating maca root into their daily routine can provide significant benefits in addressing these issues.
4. **Vitex (Chaste Tree Berry):** Vitex is one of the most well-known herbs for supporting women's reproductive health. It helps regulate hormonal balance by stimulating the pituitary gland, which in turn influences the production of estrogen and progesterone. For women with irregular menstrual cycles or those who experience symptoms of PMS, adding vitex to their herbal regimen can help create the optimal conditions for conception.
5. **Damiana:** Traditionally used as an aphrodisiac, damiana has been recognized for its ability to improve sexual desire and performance. Its positive effects on mood, stress, and

mild depression may also contribute to a more relaxed state of mind that can be vital when trying to conceive. Furthermore, Damiana can help improve circulation within the pelvic region, which may promote healthier reproductive organs.

6. **Dong Quai:** Dong quai is often referred to as "female ginseng" due to its powerful adaptogenic properties that support hormonal balance and overall vitality in women. It helps strengthen uterine muscles, regulate menstrual cycles, and alleviate PMS symptoms. Its anti-inflammatory properties may also aid in reducing endometriosis-associated pain.

7. **Black Cohosh:** Black cohosh has garnered attention for its ability to promote hormonal balance and alleviate menopausal symptoms. However, it can also benefit women who are trying to conceive by regulating menstrual cycles and reducing inflammation in the reproductive organs.

When incorporating these herbs into your routine, it is paramount that you consult with a healthcare professional or a qualified herbalist before use. This will ensure that you are using herbs safely and effectively based on your individual health needs and any pre-existing medical conditions. Using herbs as part of a holistic approach to enhancing fertility can provide tremendous benefits for women's health. These natural remedies have been trusted by generations of women seeking to optimize their reproductive functions and achieve balance within their bodies.

Healthy Pregnancy and Postpartum Recovery

Pregnancy is a beautiful and transformative journey for expectant mothers. It is a time of significant change, both physically and emotionally. Despite the challenges that come with pregnancy, following a healthy lifestyle and incorporating Dr. Sebi's herbal remedies can assist in ensuring a healthy pregnancy and postpartum recovery. In this section, we will provide guidance on nurturing your body during these important life stages using Dr. Sebi's holistic approach.

A Healthy Diet During Pregnancy

One of the essential aspects of a healthy pregnancy is maintaining a balanced diet, which nourishes not only the mother but also the developing baby. A wholesome diet provides energy, builds your baby's body, and helps prevent complications during pregnancy and childbirth. Dr. Sebi's Nutritional Guide promotes consuming alkaline, non-hybrid, and non-GMO foods to promote natural healing within the body. These include fresh fruits, vegetables, nuts, seeds, and legumes which prevent acid build-up and help create an environment that supports a healthy pregnancy. A pregnant woman's diet should contain adequate amounts of:

1. Protein: Found in hemp seeds, amaranth greens (callaloo), quinoa, mushrooms, and nuts.

2. Calcium: Abundant in sesame seeds (tahini), sea vegetables (kelp), walnuts, amaranth greens (callaloo), and kale.

3. Iron: Rich sources include sarsaparilla, dandelion root tea, figs, dates, thyme tea.

4. Folate: Obtainable from romaine lettuce, kale, broccoli rabe (rapini), avocados.

5. Vitamins: Plentiful in fruits such as guava, mangoes; vegetables like kale and bell peppers; herbs like nettle leaf tea.

Another critical component of a healthy pregnancy is regular light exercise, which strengthens muscles, enhances stamina, and improves circulation. Dr. Sebi recommended mild aerobic exercises like walking, prenatal yoga or stretching, and meditation. Remember always to listen to your body and consult your healthcare provider before starting any new exercise regimen.

Dr. Sebi's Herbal Remedies for Pregnancy

Along with proper nutrition and a balanced diet, certain herbal remedies can support women's health during pregnancy by enhancing the immune system, boosting energy levels, and alleviating common pregnancy ailments. Some recommended Dr. Sebi herbal remedies include:

1. Yellow Dock: This herb helps cleanse the blood and is known to strengthen the uterus in preparation for labor. It also assists in maintaining iron levels.

2. Red Raspberry Leaf: A popular herb among pregnant women, it strengthens the uterus, lessens morning sickness, reduces labor pains, and increases milk production during breastfeeding.

Postpartum Recovery with Dr. Sebi's Approach

The postpartum period is crucial for recovery, as the mother's body undergoes significant changes while nurturing a newborn baby. Dr. Sebi's approach to postpartum recovery emphasizes self-care through proper nutrition and herbal remedies.

A well-balanced diet is essential during the postpartum period as it accelerates healing, produces high-quality breast milk, and helps maintain energy levels with fluctuating sleep schedules. Include foods rich in iron such as dates and figs; calcium sources like sesame seeds and sea vegetables; protein from quinoa or mushrooms; vitamins from fresh fruits like papayas or kiwi fruits; and minerals like potassium from cantaloupe or coconut water.

Herbal remedies can alleviate several postpartum ailments while supporting overall healing:

1. Blue Vervain: Known as a natural tranquilizer, it helps reduce stress while promoting restful sleep.

2. Damiana: It helps uplift the mood, alleviate postpartum depression, and increased libido.

3. Lily of the Valley: This herb supports heart health by regulating blood pressure while helping to alleviate postpartum swelling.

CHAPTER 5

ENHANCING MEN'S HEALTH THROUGH HERBS

Supporting Prostate Health

Prostate health is an essential aspect of men's well-being. The prostate is a small, walnut-shaped gland in men that produces seminal fluid, which nourishes and transports sperm. Keeping the prostate healthy is crucial for maintaining proper sexual function and preventing various health issues such as prostatitis, benign prostatic hyperplasia (BPH), and prostate cancer.

It is vital to prioritize prostate health because issues with the gland can lead to severe complications if left untreated or poorly managed. Prostatitis, an inflammation of the prostate gland, can cause pain during urination or ejaculation, fever, and chills. BPH is a non-cancerous enlargement of the prostate gland that can lead to issues with urinary flow and increase the chance of urinary tract infections. On top of that, prostate cancer is one of the most common types of cancer among men. Dr. Sebi studied and researched various herbs that have shown to be effective in promoting and supporting prostate health. Below are some of these herbs and their uses:

1. Saw Palmetto: Saw palmetto is frequently used to manage BPH symptoms through its anti-inflammatory properties. It may help shrink the enlarged prostate and improve urinary flow.

2. Stinging Nettle: Stinging nettle root has been used in traditional medicine to relieve symptoms associated with an enlarged prostate, supporting overall prostate health.

3. Pygeum Africanum: Research has shown that pygeum extract can be beneficial for individuals suffering from BPH by reducing inflammation and promoting healthy urine flow.

4. Gravel Root: Gravel root has been used as a diuretic and has shown great potential in managing prostatitis and soothing urinary tract discomfort.

5. Burdock Root: Burdock root is known for its antioxidant and anti-inflammatory properties, which can contribute to overall prostate health. It can also aid in detoxifying the body, making it an excellent supplement for maintaining a healthy prostate gland.

Incorporating these herbs into your daily routine can significantly impact prostate health. It is essential to consult with a healthcare professional before starting any new herbal treatment to ensure it is suitable for your specific needs and medical history.

Apart from herbal remedies, maintaining a healthy diet is crucial for supporting prostate health. Dr. Sebi's alkaline diet promotes consuming plant-based foods that provide essential nutrients without causing inflammation in the body. Here are some dietary recommendations to promote prostate health:

1. Consume dark, leafy greens such as kale, spinach, and collard greens for their high antioxidant content.
2. Eat plenty of fruits rich in antioxidants such as berries and pomegranates.
3. Include nuts and seeds like almonds, walnuts, flax seeds, and chia seeds for their rich source of healthy fats.
4. Opt for whole grain varieties of bread, pasta, and rice to prevent spikes in blood sugar levels typically associated with processed grains.
5. Minimize consumption of processed foods, refined sugars, and unhealthy fats that can contribute to inflammation and poor prostate health.

In addition to herbal remedies and dietary changes, incorporating healthy lifestyle habits can also improve prostate health significantly:

1. Exercise regularly: Engaging in physical activities like walking, jogging or swimming can reduce the risk of developing prostate issues.

2. Maintain a healthy body weight: Obesity has been linked with an increased risk of BPH and prostate cancer. Maintaining a healthy weight through proper nutrition and exercise helps to support optimal prostate health.

3. Manage stress: Chronic stress can negatively impact overall health, including prostate health. Consider incorporating relaxation techniques such as deep breathing, meditation, or yoga into your routine.

4. Sleep well: Aim for 7-9 hours of quality sleep each night for optimal overall health and maintaining a healthy prostate.

Increasing Stamina and Endurance

For ages, men have sought ways to improve their stamina and endurance to excel in various aspects of life. Be it physical activities, sports, or personal health, possessing long-lasting endurance is crucial for achieving a well-balanced and vigorous lifestyle. Stamina and endurance are often used interchangeably; however, they possess slight differences. Stamina typically refers to the ability to sustain prolonged physical or mental activities, while endurance relates to one's capacity to withstand fatigue, hardship, or stress. Nonetheless, both stamina and endurance play an essential role in determining overall health and wellbeing.

Various factors can impact a man's stamina and endurance. Some of these influencers include diet, exercise routines, stress levels, sleep quality, and habits such as smoking or alcohol consumption. By recognizing these contributors, we can develop strategies to mitigate their detrimental effects on our endurance.

Dr. Sebi believed that using plants sourced from nature can improve human health significantly. He developed numerous herbal remedies based on this philosophy – many of which can be beneficial for increasing stamina and endurance in men's health.

1. Sarsaparilla: It has been used traditionally to treat various ailments such as skin diseases, fever, and joint pain. It contains high concentrations of antioxidants that help fight inflammation in the body. Its anti-inflammatory properties can be particularly useful for athletes or those involved in physically demanding routines - by reducing joint pain and promoting quicker recovery following intensive workouts.

2. Damiana: It is known as a natural aphrodisiac historically used by various indigenous cultures to improve sexual performance and overall energy. Aside from its libido-boosting effects, Damiana also promotes relaxation and helps alleviate anxiety and stress – two factors that can have a negative impact on both stamina and endurance.

3. Irish Sea Moss: It is a type of seaweed that contains high levels of vitamins, minerals, and essential amino acids. Due to its gelatinous consistency, it provides a natural energy boost when consumed. Additionally, its abundance in potassium chloride helps break down mucus and inflammation in the body, promoting overall stamina and improved respiratory function.

4. Gingko Biloba: This ancient tree species is known for its memory-enhancing effects but also has potential benefits for men's physical endurance. By boosting nitric oxide levels in the body, Ginkgo Biloba expands blood vessels allowing increased blood flow to muscles during exercise, subsequently enhancing athletic performance.

5. Maca Root: It is an Andean superfood that has been used by indigenous communities for centuries to improve energy levels and hormonal balance. Rich in essential nutrients such as iron, calcium, zinc, amino acids, and vitamins B1, B2, and C, Maca root can help alleviate fatigue in men while increasing overall stamina.

While herbal remedies play a significant role in building stamina and endurance in men's health, coupling these natural treatments with healthy lifestyle choices can augment lasting results.

1. Adopt a plant-based diet: Dr. Sebi encouraged followers to adhere to an alkaline plant-based diet consisting of fresh fruits, vegetables, nuts, seeds, and whole grains. These foods provide the nutrients required by the body for optimal functioning while maintaining a healthy weight.

2. Exercise regularly: Incorporating regular physical activity into your routine is crucial for enhancing endurance and stamina. Focus on exercises that target different muscle groups such as strength training and cardiovascular workouts like running or cycling.

3. Prioritize sleep: Adequate sleep is vital for muscle repair and overall health. Aim for 7-9 hours of uninterrupted sleep every night to promote optimal stamina and endurance.

4. Manage stress: Chronic stress can impede your body's ability to recover and perform at its best. Engage in stress-relief techniques such as meditation, yoga or deep breathing exercises to promote mental resilience and emotional wellbeing alongside physical strength.

5. Stay hydrated: Drinking sufficient water throughout the day is essential for regulating body temperature, preventing muscle cramps, and maintaining overall peak performance.

Herbs for Men's Sexual Vitality

Stress, poor diet, and environmental factors can all take a toll on one's libido and overall sexual health. Let's explore the powerful benefits of Dr. Sebi's herbal remedies for enhancing men's sexual vitality.

1. Damiana: Found primarily in Central and South America, Damiana is a popular herb known for its aphrodisiac properties. It has been used for centuries as a natural remedy for enhancing sexual desire, improving stamina, and increasing virility. Damiana works by improving blood flow throughout the body, particularly the genital region, making it an excellent choice for promoting overall sexual health.

2. Sarsaparilla: Rooted in ancient herbal medicine, Sarsaparilla is commonly used as a tonic for aiding both energy levels and sexual vitality. Its active compounds, known as saponins, stimulate hormone production directly linked to enhancing libido and virility. The potent antioxidants found in Sarsaparilla also help combat free radicals that may contribute to diminished sexual function.

3. Muira Puama: Originating from the Amazon rainforest, Muira Puama is often referred to as the "Viagra of the Amazon" due to its powerful potential in boosting male sexual vitality. Traditionally used as an aphrodisiac and strength enhancer, Muira Puama is believed to stimulate testosterone production and improve erection quality in men who are experiencing sexual dysfunction.

4. Tribulus Terrestris: Tribulus Terrestris, a Mediterranean plant widely known for its libido-enhancing benefits, is a popular herbal remedy among athletes and bodybuilders. Its active ingredients promote increased testosterone production and improved circulation, leading to enhanced sexual desire, stamina, and performance.

5. Maca: Maca, a native Peruvian root well-regarded for its various health benefits, has been used for centuries as both an energy booster and aphrodisiac. The high nutritional content found in Maca may help improve libido by providing essential vitamins and minerals needed to support sexual function and hormone balance.

6. Horny Goat Weed: Horny Goat Weed is an herb traditionally used in Chinese medicine for improving libido, stamina, and erectile function. The active ingredient icariin is known to increase nitric oxide levels, which in turn improves blood circulation throughout the body – crucial for healthy erectile function.

7. Saw Palmetto: Saw Palmetto is widely recognized for its prostate health benefits, but it also plays a significant role in supporting men's sexual vitality. This herb works by blocking the conversion of testosterone into dihydrotestosterone (DHT), which can contribute to declining libido, enlargement of the prostate gland, and erectile dysfunction.

8. Tongkat Ali: Tongkat Ali, also known as Malaysian Ginseng, is a potent herbal remedy used throughout Southeast Asia for enhancing male sexual vitality. By stimulating testosterone production and improving overall hormonal balance, Tongkat Ali supports increased libido, sexual performance, and sperm count in men.

9. Ginkgo Biloba: Ginkgo Biloba has long been esteemed for its cognitive enhancement properties; however, it also offers notable benefits for men's sexual health. This ancient herb works by increasing blood circulation throughout the body – including the genital region – which is vital for robust erectile function.

10. Yohimbe: Yohimbe is an African tree bark extract known for its stimulating and aphrodisiacal effects. The active compound, yohimbine, is believed to help treat erectile dysfunction by increasing blood flow to the penile region, allowing for stronger and more consistent erections.

Incorporating these powerful herbs into your daily regimen can provide a safe and natural way to enhance sexual vitality and reclaim the intimate connection that may have waned over time. It is important to consult with a healthcare professional before beginning any new herbal supplement, especially if you are currently taking medications or have pre-existing health conditions.

CHAPTER 6

HERBAL WELLNESS FOR CHILDREN AND ELDERS

Gentle Herbs for Children's Ailments

In this section, we will explore the gentle and effective herbal remedies outlined by Dr. Sebi to treat common ailments that children may experience. As parents or caregivers, it is vital to approach our children's health holistically and prioritize natural healing methods whenever possible.

1. Chamomile: Chamomile is a mild yet potent herb that soothes and calms both the body and mind. It has been popularly used in various cultures for centuries due to its ability to alleviate symptoms of various conditions such as colds, fevers, restlessness, and stomach aches. To administer chamomile to your child, brew a warm cup of chamomile tea using dried flowers or a tea bag. Make sure the tea is not too hot before offering it to your child.

2. Elderberry: Elderberries are another essential herb in the Dr. Sebi Herbal Bible, which can be highly beneficial for children suffering from cold, flu, and upper respiratory infections. Rich in antioxidants and vitamin C, elderberry syrup can be an asset in supporting and strengthening the immune system. You can give your child store-bought elderberry syrup or create your homemade version using dried elderberries.

3. Ginger: Ginger is a time-tested remedy for digestive issues such as nausea, bloating, gas, and upset stomachs. It also has anti-inflammatory properties that help reduce pain and inflammation associated with illnesses like arthritis or joint pain. Giving ginger tea or adding fresh ginger juice to a glass of lukewarm water can help alleviate many of these symptoms for children.

4. Peppermint: Peppermint has been utilized for centuries for its cooling effect on the body and its ability to calm irritated skin. It can be used in various ways - either topically or ingested orally by children. Peppermint oil can be diluted with a carrier oil and applied to the skin for itch relief, while warm peppermint tea can offer relief from stomach aches and nausea.

70

5. Mullein: Mullein is an essential herb for respiratory health, as it helps clear mucus from the lungs. Thus, this herb is beneficial for children with bronchitis, asthma, or other respiratory infections. You can prepare mullein tea by steeping the dried leaves in hot water for 10-15 mins or purchase a ready-made tincture to administer to your child.

6. Eucalyptus: Eucalyptus is well-known for its use in treating colds and congestion in children. Rich in antimicrobial properties, eucalyptus essential oil can be added to a humidifier or mixed with a carrier oil and massaged on the child's chest to provide relief from respiratory issues. Ensure that you always dilute eucalyptus oil with a carrier oil and do not apply it directly on the child's skin.

7. Aloe Vera: Aloe Vera is another fantastic plant featured in Dr. Sebi's Herbal Bible, which offers numerous benefits for children's health. Aloe gel can treat burns, small cuts, abrasions, and skin conditions like eczema due to its moisturizing and soothing properties. Additionally, consuming aloe vera juice can alleviate digestive discomfort and provide essential nutrients.

8. Lavender: Lavender is praised for its calming effects and ability to reduce anxiety, stress, and tension, which makes it an excellent remedy for children struggling with sleep or restlessness issues. Inhaling lavender essential oil diffused into space can create a tranquil environment conducive to relaxation and restful sleep in your child's room.

Parents and caregivers should be proactive in their approach to maintaining and enhancing their child's health using these natural remedies. Always remember to consult a professional herbalist or healthcare provider before administering or adjusting any herbal treatment for your child, especially if they have existing medical conditions, are taking medication, or are under the age of two.

Strengthening Elder Immunity

As we age, our bodies undergo various changes that can impact the strength and efficiency of our immune systems. This becomes increasingly true for seniors, who may struggle with staying healthy and warding off illnesses. Growing older can lead to a weakened immune system, which is especially at-risk during flu and cold seasons. With weakened immunity, seniors become more susceptible to infections and their complications. Strengthening elder immunity is crucial to ensure a robust defense against illness and enhance overall wellbeing.

The Dr. Sebi method is an enduring testament to the power of natural, plant-based remedies in promoting health and addressing various health conditions. Based on the concept of utilizing nutrient-dense alkaline foods and herbs native to Africa and the Caribbean, Dr. Sebi's approach aims to detoxify our bodies and restore its natural ability to self-heal.

To incorporate Dr. Sebi's method into your daily life as a senior citizen, focus on consuming alkaline, nutrient-rich foods that are free from genetically modified organisms (GMOs), pesticides, herbicides, and other toxic substances. Aim for a balanced diet including the following alkaline meal essentials:

1. Leafy Greens: Rich sources like kale, dandelion greens, turnip greens, and watercress are high in immune-boosting vitamins A, C, E, and K.

2. Fruits: Enjoy seasonal fruits such as apples, berries, bananas, grapes, and papayas that contain antioxidants to protect your immune system.

3. Nuts and Seeds: Raw almonds or walnuts, along with chia, hemp, and sesame seeds, provide beneficial fats, proteins and essential minerals for improved immune function.

4. Whole Grains: Opt for grains such as quinoa, wild rice, or spelt to ensure a good intake of fiber and minerals that can promote a healthy gut, which is critical to proper immune function.

5. Fresh Herbs: Incorporate herbs like oregano, thyme, basil, or cilantro into your meals for added flavor and potent antimicrobial and immune-boosting properties.

In addition to consuming an alkaline diet based on whole foods, consider incorporating some of Dr. Sebi's favorite herbs for elder immunity:

1. Echinacea: This herb is well-known for its ability to stimulate white blood cells and support healthy immune function. As a senior citizen, you may benefit from taking echinacea in the form of supplements or herbal tea during cold and flu seasons.

2. Elderberry: Known as a staple in traditional herbal medicine systems worldwide, elderberry has been gaining recognition for its potent antiviral properties. It can help reduce symptoms when taken at the onset of a cold or flu.

3. Sarsaparilla: This root is rich in anti-inflammatory compounds that can help maintain overall health by reducing inflammation throughout the body.

4. Irish Sea Moss: A powerful source of essential nutrients such as amino acids and iodine, Irish sea moss supports thyroid health which can positively impact immunity.

In tandem with diet modifications and herbal remedies, several lifestyle changes can aid in enhancing elder immunity:

1. **Stay Active:** Participate in regular physical activity such as walking or low-impact exercises to keep your mind and body engaged.

2. **Proper Hydration:** Ensure adequate water intake to prevent dehydration and assist in flushing toxins from the body.

3. **Adequate Sleep:** Prioritize restful sleep to support immune function, as the body repairs itself during this time.

4. **Social Interactions:** Engage in meaningful connections with family and friends to maintain positive emotional health and reduce stress, which contributes to a healthy immune system.

By incorporating Dr. Sebi's teachings on alkaline, plant-based nutrition, herbal remedies, and a balanced lifestyle, seniors have the potential to strengthen their immunity and live long, vibrant lives.

Encouraging Wellness through Family Traditions

Family traditions are the backbone of a strong and healthy family. They foster connections, create memories, and have the power to shape individual lifestyles. The *"Dr. Sebi Herbal Bible"* acknowledges the importance of incorporating wellness through plant-based healing practices into family traditions. By doing so, families can cultivate a holistic approach to health and set future generations on a path toward optimal wellbeing.

The life and teachings of Dr. Sebi revolve around using natural herbs and an alkaline diet to heal the body. This section will delve into the benefits of incorporating these principles into family traditions, as well as providing practical tips for successfully implementing them in your daily life.

1. **Creating Alkaline Family Meals:** A significant part of Dr. Sebi's recommendations is focused on consuming an alkaline diet that consists of plant-based whole foods. Preparing family meals together not only strengthens bonds but helps reinforce the importance of maintaining a wholesome diet. Selecting meals from Dr. Sebi's approved food list ensures that you are exposing your children to nutrient-dense meals which contribute to their overall wellness.

Try incorporating Dr. Sebi approved fruits, vegetables, grains, and legumes in your daily meals and experiment with new recipes as a family tradition. Teach children how to cook these healthful dishes and emphasize the benefits associated with each ingredient.

2. Growing a Family Herbal Garden: There is immense power in reconnecting with nature through plants; they have historically been our healers, nourishers, and protectors. Starting a family herbal garden is an excellent way to introduce Dr. Sebi's holistic approach while staying true to his emphasis on organic ingredients.

Choose herbs such as dandelion, burdock root, sarsaparilla, elderberry, and sea moss – all recommended by Dr. Sebi for their healing properties – to cultivate in your garden. This activity encourages teamwork and offers an opportunity to educate family members about the medicinal properties of these herbs. As seasons change, harvesting and drying herbs together can become a cherished family tradition with long-lasting health benefits.

3. Herbal Tea Rituals: Incorporate an evening herbal tea ritual into your family routine. Use the herbs you have grown in your garden or select from Dr. Sebi's approved list to brew healing, alkaline teas for everyone to enjoy. Not only will this practice introduce children to different flavors and benefits of herbal teas, but it also provides a moment for relaxation and reflection as a family unit. This daily bonding experience can contribute to improved mental and emotional health as well.

4. Wellness-themed Storytime: Instill a love of learning about wellness from an early age by incorporating wellness-themed story times into your family routine. Read books on Dr. Sebi's principles, plant-based nutrition, and the healing power of nature to help foster curiosity in your children about holistic living.

5. Visiting Nature as a Family: Set aside time for outdoor adventures as a family. Whether it's exploring local forests, hiking trails, or secluded beaches, spending time in nature helps strengthen physical and mental wellbeing while allowing you to bond with one another. During these excursions, teach children how to identify various plants that are beneficial for their health.

6. Volunteering at Community Gardens or Wellness Centers: Teach the importance of giving back by volunteering at community gardens or wellness centers focused on holistic healing or sustainable living together as a family. In doing so, you will not only aid your community but also ensure that your children understand the benefits of applying Dr. Sebi's teachings in the real world.

Creating wellness-focused family traditions is an invaluable gift that will have an impact on your loved ones for generations to come. By implementing Dr. Sebi's principles in these traditions, families can embrace a natural, plant-based approach to healing, promoting physical and emotional health that will endure throughout their lives.

BOOK 3: FROM GARDEN TO KITCHEN: GROWING & UTILIZING HERBS

CHAPTER 1

GROWING YOUR HERBAL GARDEN

Selecting, Planting, and Caring for Dr. Sebi Approved Herbs

Dr. Sebi's Herbal Bible offers an extensive list of herbs approved by the renowned holistic practitioner for their powerful medicinal properties. These herbs, when used correctly, can aid in healing various ailments and promoting optimal health. This section will guide you through the process of selecting, planting, and caring for Dr. Sebi approved herbs to create your herbal garden.

Selecting the Right Herbs

To get started, research which Dr. Sebi's herbs are most suitable for your needs. Consider any health issues or wellness goals you have and find herbs known for targeting these areas. Also, take into account the climate you live in, as some herbs may thrive better than others in your local conditions. Some popular examples of Dr. Sebi approved herbs include:

1. **Burdock Root:** Known for its blood-purifying properties and being rich in vitamins and minerals.

2. **Sarsaparilla:** Used to treat skin diseases, rheumatism, and digestive disorders.

3. **Dandelion:** Renowned for liver detoxification and diuretic properties.

4. **Sea Moss:** Packed with nutrients and minerals, it aids digestion and boosts immune function.

Planting Your Selected Herbs

Now that you've chosen your herbs, it's time to plant them. Follow these steps to ensure their success:

1. **Choose a Location:** Pick a spot in your garden that receives adequate sunlight (6–8 hours a day) and has well-draining soil.

2. **Prepare the Soil:** Amend heavy soils with organic matter (such as compost or aged manure) to improve drainage and nutrient content.

3. Decide on Seeds or Seedlings: You can either plant seeds purchased online or from a local supplier or buy seedlings from a nursery.

4. Sow the Seeds or Plant Seedlings: Follow the specific guidelines for each herb, as they vary in terms of planting depths and spacing.

5. Water Consistently: Ensure that your herbs are well-watered but not over-watered, as this can cause root rot.

Caring for Your Herbs

To keep your Dr. Sebi approved herbs healthy and productive, follow these tips:

1. Watering: Most herbs require watering once every few days or when the soil is dry to touch. Over-watering can be as detrimental as under-watering them.

2. Fertilizing: Generally, herbs don't need heavy fertilization. You can add a slow-release organic fertilizer or compost to provide additional nutrients as needed.

3. Weeding: Regularly remove any weeds from your garden bed to prevent competition for nutrients and water.

4. Pest Control: Keep an eye out for pests like aphids, snails, and slugs. Use natural methods of pest control like neem oil or introduce beneficial predator insects (e.g., ladybugs) into your garden.

5. Pruning & Harvesting: Regularly prune and harvest your herbs to encourage new growth and avoid overcrowding in the garden bed.

By following these simple steps, you'll have a flourishing Dr. Sebi approved herbal garden that provides you with an abundant supply of health-boosting plants for achieving optimal well-being.

Tips for Long-Term Success

Maintaining a successful herbal garden takes time and effort, but it's well worth the investment in promoting better health and wellness.

1. Continuously Learn: Enhance your knowledge by reading books and articles about herbs, attending workshops or webinars, or joining local gardening clubs or online groups targeting Dr. Sebi's principles.

2. Experiment with New Herbs: As you become more proficient at growing Dr. Sebi approved herbs, consider cultivating new varieties to expand your herbal repertoire.

3. Rotate Plantings: Rotate crops to prevent depletion of soil nutrients and the occurrence of pests and diseases.

4. Teach Others: Share your knowledge and experiences with friends, family members, or neighbors who may be interested in growing their herbal gardens.

Selecting, planting, and caring for Dr. Sebi approved herbs is a rewarding endeavor that not only brings therapeutic plants within your reach but also contributes to a healthier lifestyle. By following these guidelines and remaining patient and diligent, you can cultivate a vibrant herbal garden that promotes optimal well-being and healing.

Creating A Healing Space: Indoor and Outdoor Herb Gardens

Herbs have been used for centuries as natural remedies for various ailments, illnesses, and conditions. They hold incredible healing power due to their nutrition, minerals, and medicinal properties. By including herbs in our daily lives, one can experience higher energy levels, improved digestion, and overall better health. Creating your own herb garden is an excellent way to make these healing plants readily available and become a source of nourishment. The process of growing herbs also offers therapeutic benefits by connecting you with nature and serving as a meditative escape from our increasingly busy lives.

Indoor Herb Gardens

For those who have limited outdoor space or live in a location with harsh weather conditions, indoor herb gardens provide the perfect solution to incorporate healing herbs into your daily life. Indoor herb gardens can be as simple or intricate as you choose, making it easy to start small and expand over time. When choosing which herbs to grow indoors, it's essential to consider the plants' growth habits and requirements. Some herbs thrive in indoor environments, while others may require more sunlight or humidity than can be provided inside your home. Dr. Sebi recommends alkaline herbs like burdock root, sarsaparilla, elderberry, bladderwrack, Irish moss, and dandelion for optimal health benefits.

Creating an indoor herbal garden begins with selecting a space with access to natural light. South-facing windows are ideal, as they provide ample sunlight throughout the day. You can also use grow lights to supplement natural light if needed.

Next, choose your growing containers. Dr. Sebi recommends using non-toxic, earth-friendly containers like terracotta pots or wooden planters, which promote proper moisture and airflow. Additionally, select a high-quality organic potting mix that is compatible with your chosen herbs.

When planting your herbs, ensure that each plant has enough space for its roots to grow and develop properly. Most herbs should be watered when the soil's top inch becomes dry to maintain adequate moisture levels.

Outdoor Herb Gardens

If you have more outdoor space available or prefer gardening in nature, an outdoor herb garden might be the perfect choice for you. This type of garden often requires more planning and maintenance but can support a wider variety of healing plants and create a truly magical and healing environment. When creating an outdoor herb garden, consider your local climate conditions and available sunlight before choosing which herbs to grow. Dr. Sebi suggests planting alkaline herbs like blue vervain, chaparral, rhubarb root, red clover, and nettles in addition to those recommended for indoor gardens.

Design your outdoor herb garden to optimize the growth of each unique plant. Some herbs may require more sunlight than others or prefer well-draining soil. Organize your garden by placing sun-loving plants together in one area while providing partial shade or more moisture for other plants as needed.

Incorporating pathways between rows of herbs using materials such as gravel, wood chips, or stepping stones will create an inviting space perfect for meditation and reflection.

Maintaining Your Herb Gardens

Regularly care for your indoor or outdoor herb garden to ensure the plants remain healthy and productive. Foster growth by pruning overly long stems, removing dead leaves, and providing sufficient water and nutrient-rich soil.

Creating a healing herb garden is an excellent way to foster self-care and holistic wellness practices. By growing your own herbs indoors or outdoors, you have complete control over the quality and composition of your healing plants, which can be incorporated into your daily life in various forms such as teas, tinctures, or topical applications. Reap the benefits of these healing plants and bring balance to your physical, mental, and spiritual well-being with your very own herb garden sanctuary.

Harvesting and Storing Herbs for Potency

This section will provide you with insights on identifying the apt time for harvesting, the correct techniques for cutting and gathering, and tips for storing herbs to maintain their optimal potency. The optimal harvesting time for each herb depends on multiple factors like growing conditions, climate, and the part of the herb that we desire to use. Here are some general guidelines to follow:

1. Most herbs are best harvested just before they flower as this is when their essential oil content is highest.
2. Harvesting should be done early in the morning, once the dew has dried but before the sun hits its peak. This ensures that the essential oils remain intact.
3. Annual herbs can be harvested several times throughout their growing season while perennial herbs can be cut back by one-third at a time, allowing them to regrow.

Once you've identified the appropriate time for harvesting your herbal plants, utilize these simple tips:

1. Use clean and sharp scissors or shears to ensure that clean cuts are made, minimizing any damage caused to your plants.
2. Collect healthy leaves from both young and mature growths. While older leaves may have a stronger flavor profile, young leaves tend to be more tender.
3. If you're harvesting flowers or seeds, wait till they reach full maturity before picking.
4. Remove any damaged or dead plant material during harvest as it can negatively impact the potency of your herbs.

Drying: Preserve Your Harvest

Drying is a widely used method that allows you to preserve your herbs while enhancing their potency. Here's how you can dry your harvest effectively:

1. Bundle your herbs by tying a string or rubber band around the stems. Hang these bundles upside-down in a dark, well-ventilated room to maintain their color and essential oil content.
2. Ensure that sufficient airflow is maintained around the herbs to prevent any mold or mildew from forming.
3. Keep an eye on the humidity levels in the room, as high humidity can prolong the drying process.

4. It's crucial that you don't rush this process – slow drying over one to three weeks will result in more potent herbs.

Storing: Prolong Potency

Once your herbs are thoroughly dried, it is time to store them properly to ensure they maintain their potency. Follow these storage tips:

1. Store your herbs in airtight containers like glass jars or ziplock bags. This reduces the exposure of your herbs to air and prevents oxidation.
2. Label each jar or bag with the name of the herb and the date of harvest, so that you can keep track of freshness.
3. Keep these containers away from sunlight and moisture to prevent degradation caused by UV rays or dampness.
4. Opt for storing your herbs whole rather than crushing them since crushed herbs have a larger surface area exposed to air and can lose their potency faster.

By practicing these harvesting techniques and ensuring proper storage, you will be one step closer to enjoying Dr. Sebi's herbal remedies at their full potency! The care you take during this stage will make all the difference in the effectiveness of the remedies you create using these potent plants.

CHAPTER 2

ALKALINE HERBAL RECIPES

Breakfast, Lunch, And Dinner Recipes Following Dr. Sebi's Guidelines

Spelt Pancakes with Agave Syrup (Breakfast)

Preparation time: Ten mins

Cooking time: Fifteen mins

Servings: Four

Ingredients:

- One & half cups spelt flour
- Two tbsp agave syrup
- Two cups walnut milk
- One tsp sea salt
- Two tbsp grapeseed oil

Directions:

1. In your big container, mix spelt flour plus sea salt.
2. In another container, mix walnut milk plus two tbsp oil. Combine it with flour mixture till blended.
3. Warm up your big non-stick skillet on moderate temp, then add some grapeseed oil.
4. Pour batter onto your skillet, then cook within two to three mins per side till golden brown. Top with agave syrup, then serve.

Nutritional Values (per serving): Calories: 340; Carbs: 52g; Fat: 12g; Protein: 9g

Alkaline Blueberry Smoothie (Breakfast)

Preparation time: Ten mins

Cooking time: Zero mins

Servings: Two

Ingredients:

- One cup fresh organic blueberries
- One medium ripe burro banana, chopped
- Half of an avocado
- Two cups fresh coconut water
- Half tsp ground sea moss

Directions:

1. In your blender, mix blueberries, banana, avocado flesh, coconut water, plus ground sea moss.
2. Blend till smooth. Serve.

Nutritional Values (per serving): Calories: 310; Carbs: 45g; Fat: 15g; Protein: 8g

Amaranth Porridge with Berries (Breakfast)

Preparation time: Fifteen mins

Cooking time: Twenty mins

Servings: Four

Ingredients:

- One cup amaranth, washed
- Two cups spring water
- One tbsp agave syrup
- Half tsp sea salt
- One cup mixed berries
- One tbsp grapeseed oil
- One tsp ground cinnamon
- Half tsp ground nutmeg

Directions:

1. In your medium saucepan, let spring water boil, then add amaranth. Adjust to low temp, then cook within twenty mins, mixing often till creamy.
2. In your separate pan on moderate temp, add grapeseed oil plus mixed berries. Cook within five to seven mins till berries are softened.
3. Mix in agave syrup, sea salt, cinnamon, plus nutmeg to your cooked amaranth. Serve the warm amaranth porridge topped with cooked berries.

Nutritional Values (per serving): Calories: 210; Carbs: 38g; Fat: 5g; Protein: 6g

Kamut Veggie Scramble (Breakfast)

Preparation time: Fifteen mins

Cooking time: Twenty mins

Servings: Four

Ingredients:

- One cup kamut grains, pre-soaked overnight & strained
- Two tbsp grapeseed oil
- Half cup chopped each green & red bell pepper
- Half cup cup chopped yellow onion
- One cup sliced mushrooms
- Three cups chopped kale or spinach
- Half tsp sea salt
- Quarter tsp each cayenne pepper & crushed oregano

Directions:

1. Warm up two tbsp oil in your big skillet on moderate temp. Add kamut grains, then cook within ten mins, mixing often, till slightly golden-brown.
2. Add bell peppers, plus onion, then sauté within five mins till vegetables are tender. Add mushrooms, kale, sea salt, cayenne pepper, plus crushed oregano. Mix well.
3. Cook within three to five mins till the kale has wilted. Serve.

Nutritional Values (per serving): Calories: 280; Carbs: 40g; Fat: 10g; Protein: 10g

Walnut Hemp Seed Granola (Breakfast)

Preparation time: Fifteen mins

Cooking time: Thirty mins

Servings: Eight

Ingredients:

- One & half cups walnut pieces
- Three-fourths cup hemp seeds
- Half cup unsweetened shredded coconut
- Quarter cup each agave syrup & grapeseed oil
- One tsp sea salt
- Half tsp ground cinnamon

Directions:

1. Warm up your oven to 325°F.
2. In your big container, mix walnuts, hemp seeds, plus shredded coconut.
3. In your separate container, whisk agave syrup, oil, sea salt, plus ground cinnamon. Combine it with walnut mixture till blended.
4. Spread granola mixture onto your lined baking sheet. Bake within fifteen mins. Mix well, then bake again within fifteen mins till crispy. Remove, cool it down, then serve.

Nutritional Values (per serving): Calories: 420; Carbs: 16g; Fat: 37g; Protein: 13g;

Quinoa Stuffed Bell Peppers (Lunch)

Preparation time: Fifteen mins

Cooking time: Forty-five mins

Servings: Four

Ingredients:

- One cup uncooked quinoa, washed
- Two cups spring water
- Four medium bell peppers, sliced tops & seeded
- One tbsp grapeseed oil

- One small red onion, finely chopped
- Two cloves of fresh garlic, minced
- One cup cherry tomatoes, halved
- Half cup diced zucchini
- Half cup chopped fresh basil
- One tsp sea salt

Directions:

1. Put quinoa plus spring water in your medium saucepan. Let it boil, adjust to low temp, cover, then simmer within fifteen mins. Fluff using your fork, then put aside.
2. Warm up your oven to 375°F. Put bell peppers in your baking dish. Warm up oil in your skillet on moderate temp. Add red onion plus garlic, then cook till soft.
3. Mix in cherry tomatoes, zucchini, plus cooked quinoa within five mins.
4. Add basil plus sea salt, mixing well. Fill each bell pepper using quinoa mixture. Cover using aluminum foil, then bake stuffed peppers within thirty-five mins till tender. Serve.

Nutritional Values (per serving): Calories 280; Carbs 51g; Fat 6g; Protein 11g

Chickpea Avocado Salad (Lunch)

Preparation time: Fifteen mins

Cooking time: Zero mins

Servings: Four

Ingredients:

- Two cups cooked chickpeas
- One big avocado, diced
- One medium red bell pepper, chopped
- Half cup chopped each red onion & cucumber
- Quarter cup fresh cilantro, chopped
- Two tbsp lime juice
- Three tbsp grapeseed oil
- Sea salt & cayenne pepper, as required

Directions:

1. In your big container, mix cooked chickpeas, avocado, bell pepper, onion, plus cucumber.

2. In your small container, whisk lime juice plus grapeseed oil. Drizzle it over your salad, then mix gently. Flavor it using sea salt and cayenne pepper. Fold in cilantro, then serve.

Nutritional Values (per serving): Calories 356; Carbs 35g; Fat 20g; Protein 10g

Grilled Portobello Mushroom Burgers (Lunch)

Preparation time: Fifteen mins

Cooking time: Ten mins

Servings: Four

Ingredients:

- Four big portobello mushroom caps
- Quarter cup grapeseed oil
- Two tbsp fresh lime juice
- One tbsp agave syrup
- One tsp sea salt
- Half tsp cayenne pepper
- Four spelt flour burger buns, toasted
- One avocado, sliced
- One bunch of arugula
- One small red onion, thinly sliced

Directions:

1. In your shallow dish, whisk oil, lime juice, agave syrup, sea salt, plus cayenne pepper. Mix in mushroom caps, then let them to sit within ten mins, turning often.

2. Warm up your grill to moderate-high temp. Cook marinated mushroom caps within five mins per side till tender.

3. Put one grilled portobello mushroom cap on each bun bottom, then add avocado, arugula, and onion. Cover using your bun tops, then serve.

Nutritional Values (per serving): Calories 446; Carbs 43g; Fat 24g; Protein 7g

Alkaline Wrap with Wild Arugula (Lunch)

Preparation time: Fifteen mins

Cooking time: Twenty mins

Servings: Four wraps

Ingredients:

- Two cups wild arugula
- One cup kamut flour
- One tsp sea salt
- One cup spring water
- One tbsp grapeseed oil
- One cup sliced bell peppers
- Half cup sliced red onions
- Half cup chopped cherry tomatoes
- Half cup diced cucumbers
- Half avocado, thinly sliced

Directions:

1. In your container, add kamut flour plus sea salt, then slowly pour in your spring water. Mix till a dough form.
2. Split it into four, then roll each into a ball. Flatten each ball on your clean surface to create four wrap-sized circles.
3. Warm up your non-stick pan on medium temp, then add grapeseed oil. Cook one wrap within two to three mins per side till slightly browned. Repeat using rest of wraps.
4. In another pan, sauté bell peppers plus onions within five mins till tender. Put aside.
5. Fill each wrap using wild arugula, bell peppers, onions, cherry tomatoes, cucumbers, plus avocado slices. Fold in sides of wraps to enclose filling. Serve.

Nutritional Values (per serving): Calories 280; Carbs 37g; Fat 11g; Protein 8g

Dr. Sebi's Butternut Squash Soup (Lunch)

Preparation time: Fifteen mins

Cooking time: Forty-five mins

Servings: Four

Ingredients:

- One medium butternut squash, peeled, seeded, & chopped
- One tbsp grapeseed oil
- One small red onion, chopped
- Two cloves of fresh garlic, minced
- One small burro banana, sliced
- Four cups of spring water
- One tsp sea salt

Directions:

1. In your big pot, warm up oil on moderate temp. Put onion plus garlic, then cook within five to seven mins till onions are translucent.
2. Add butternut squash plus burro banana, then cook within ten more mins, mixing often. Pour in the spring water, then flavor it using sea salt.
3. Let it boil, cover, then adjust to a simmer. Cook within thirty mins till butternut squash is tender.
4. Blend soup using your immersion blender till smooth. Warm it up again, then serve.

Nutritional Values (per serving): Calories: 180; Carbs: 40g; Fat: 4g; Protein: 4g

Sebi's Eggplant Zucchini Casserole (Dinner)

Preparation time: Fifteen mins

Cooking time: One hour

Servings: Six

Ingredients:

- Two medium each zucchinis & eggplants, sliced into half-inch rounds
- One cup cherry tomatoes, halved
- One cup fresh basil leaves, chopped
- One red bell pepper, deseeded & chopped
- Half cup spring onions, chopped
- One tsp sea salt
- Two tbsp grapeseed oil

Directions:

1. Warm up your oven to 350°F. Arrange half of your eggplants and zucchinis in your oven-safe casserole dish.
2. Mix cherry tomatoes, bell pepper, spring onions, plus basil in your container. Flavor it using sea salt, then mix well.
3. Spread it on your arranged eggplant and zucchini slices. Layer rest of eggplant and zucchini slices on top.
4. Drizzle two tbsp oil on your layered casserole. Cover using your aluminum foil, then bake within forty-five mins.
5. Uncover, then bake within fifteen mins till golden brown. Serve.

Nutritional Values (per serving): Calories: 92; Carbs: 13g; Fat: 3g; Protein: 3g

Stuffed Romaine Boats with Mushroom Sauce (Dinner)

Preparation time: Fifteen mins

Cooking time: Twenty-five mins

Servings: Four

Ingredients:

- Four large romaine lettuce leaves
- Two cups chopped mushrooms
- One cup diced bell peppers
- Half cup diced red onion
- One tbsp grapeseed oil
- One tbsp fresh thyme leaves
- Half tsp sea salt
- Quarter tsp cayenne pepper
- Half cup crushed walnuts

For the Mushroom Sauce:

- One cup chopped mushrooms
- Two cups spring water
- One tbsp grapeseed oil
- Half tsp sea salt

- Quarter tsp cayenne pepper

Directions:

1. In your big skillet, warm up oil on moderate temp. Add bell peppers plus onion, then cook within five mins till they become soft.
2. Mix in mushrooms, thyme, sea salt, plus cayenne pepper. Cook within ten mins till mushrooms are tender.
3. For your mushroom sauce, blend mushrooms, spring water, oil, sea salt, and cayenne pepper in your blender till smooth.
4. Warm up mushroom sauce in your saucepan on low temp within five mins. Fill each romaine lettuce leaf using cooked vegetable-mushroom mixture.
5. Top each lettuce boat using walnuts. Drizzle warm mushroom sauce on each romaine boat. Serve.

Nutritional Values (per serving): Calories 200; Carbs 10g; Fat 15g; Protein 7g

Spicy Quinoa and Kale Curry (Dinner)

Preparation time: Fifteen mins

Cooking time: Thirty mins

Servings: Four

Ingredients:

- One cup raw quinoa, washed & strained
- Two cups kale, chopped
- Two tbsp grapeseed oil
- Half red onion, chopped
- One red bell pepper, chopped
- Three cloves of fresh garlic, minced
- One tsp ground each coriander & cayenne pepper
- Half tsp sea salt
- Two cups vegetable broth
- One cup coconut milk
- Juice of one key lime

Directions:

1. In your medium pot, warm up oil on moderate temp. Add onion plus bell pepper, then cook within five mins till softened. Mix in garlic, then cook within one min.
2. Add quinoa, then mix well. Flavor it using coriander, cayenne pepper, plus sea salt. Pour broth, mixing well. Let it boil, adjust to a simmer, then cover it within twenty mins.
3. Mix in coconut milk plus kale, then cook within five mins till kale wilts slightly. Remove, then squeeze lime juice on top. Serve.

Nutritional Values (per serving): Calories: 259; Carbs: 37g; Fat: 9g; Protein: 8g

Almond Crusted Cauliflower Tacos (Dinner)

Preparation time: Twenty mins

Cooking time: Thirty mins

Servings: Four

Ingredients:

- One medium cauliflower head, broken into florets
- Two cups almond flour
- One cup spelt flour
- One cup spring water
- Two tbsp seamoss gel
- One tbsp ground each cayenne pepper & paprika
- One tbsp onion powder
- One tbsp oregano, dried
- Two tsp sea salt
- Two tsp grapeseed oil
- Eight spelt tortillas, warmed

Directions:

1. Warm up your oven to 375°F.
2. In your big container, mix flours, seamoss gel, cayenne, paprika, onion powder, oregano, plus one tsp sea salt.
3. Slowly add spring water, then mix till smooth. Dip each cauliflower floret into your batter.

4. Put coated florets onto your lined baking sheet, then drizzle using oil. Bake within thirty mins till cauliflower is crispy.
5. Put two or three baked cauliflower florets onto each warmed tortilla. Serve.

Nutritional Values (per serving): Calories: 489; Carbs: 55g; Fat: 25g; Protein: 15g

Brazilian Sea Moss Pepper Pot (Dinner)

Preparation time: Fifteen mins

Cooking time: Forty-five mins

Servings: Four

Ingredients:

- One cup dried sea moss, soaked & washed
- One tbsp grapeseed oil
- One medium yellow onion, diced
- Three cloves of garlic, minced
- One small each green & red bell pepper, diced
- Two cups vegetable broth (Dr. Sebi approved)
- One cup chopped kale
- Two tsp thyme, chopped
- One tsp oregano, chopped
- One bay leaf
- Sea salt & crushed black pepper, as required

Directions:

1. Warm up oil in your big pot on moderate temp. Add onion, garlic, plus bell peppers, then cook within five mins till vegetables are soft.
2. Add sea moss plus broth, let it boil, then adjust to a simmer. Add bay leaf, thyme, oregano, salt, plus black pepper.
3. Cover, then let it simmer within thirty mins till the sea moss turns tender. Add your kale, then simmer within ten mins. Serve.

Nutritional Values (per serving): Calories: 120; Carbs: 18g; Fat: 3g; Protein: 4g

Herbal Blends for Specific Health Concerns

Immunity Boosting Ginger and Key Lime Tea

Preparation time: Ten mins

Cooking time: Fifteen mins

Servings: Four

Ingredients:

- Two tbsp grated ginger
- Four cups spring water
- One tbsp dried soursop leaves (optional)
- Four key limes, juiced & zested
- Two tbsp agave syrup
- Sea salt, as required

Directions:

1. In your medium saucepan, mix ginger, spring water, plus dried soursop leaves (if using). Let it boil on moderate-high temp.
2. Adjust to low temp, then let it simmer within ten mins. Remove your saucepan, then strain your liquid. Mix in juice, zest, agave syrup, plus sea salt. Serve.

Nutritional Values (per serving): Calories: 40; Carbs: 10g; Fat: 0g; Protein: 0g

Anti-Inflammatory Burdock Root and Sarsaparilla Tea Blend

Preparation time: Ten mins

Cooking time: Thirty mins

Servings: Four

Ingredients:

- One tbsp burdock root, coarsely chopped
- One tbsp sarsaparilla root, coarsely chopped
- Four cups spring water
- Two tbsp agave syrup (optional)

Directions:

1. In your medium saucepan, mix burdock root, sarsaparilla root, plus spring water. Let it boil on moderate-high temp.
2. Adjust to low temp, then simmer within thirty mins. Remove your saucepan, then let your tea steep within ten mins.
3. Strain, if desired, sweeten your tea using agave syrup. Serve.

Nutritional Values (per serving): Calories 15; Carbs 3g; Fat 0g; Protein 0g

Digestive-Soothing Chamomile-Fennel Tea

Preparation time: Five mins

Cooking time: Ten mins

Servings: Two

Ingredients:

- One tbsp dried chamomile flowers
- One tbsp crushed fennel seeds
- Four cups spring water
- Two tsp agave syrup (optional)
- One pinch of sea moss powder (optional)

Directions:

1. In your small pot, mix dried chamomile flowers plus crushed fennel seeds.
2. Pour in spring water, then warm it up on moderate temp. Simmer within ten mins. Strain, if desired, sweeten your tea using agave syrup.
3. You can also add a pinch of sea moss powder for additional minerals. Mix well, then serve.

Nutritional Values (per serving): Calories 23; Carbs 0.6g; Fat 0g; Protein 0.2g

Energy-Enhancing Burdock-Guayusa Tea

Preparation time: Five mins

Cooking time: Twenty mins

Servings: Four

Ingredients:

- Four cups filtered water
- One tbsp dried each burdock root & guayusa leaves
- Two tbsp agave syrup
- One tbsp fresh lime juice

Directions:

1. In your medium saucepan, let filtered water boil. Add dried burdock root plus guayusa leaves.
2. Adjust to low temp, cover, then simmer within fifteen mins. Strain into your pitcher.
3. Mix in agave syrup plus lime juice. Serve.

Nutritional Values (per serving): Calories 90; Carbs 20g; Fat 0g; Protein 2g

Calming Chamomile & Linden Tea

Preparation time: Five mins

Cooking time: Ten mins

Servings: Four

Ingredients:

- Quarter cup dried chamomile flowers
- Quarter cup dried linden flowers
- Four cups spring water
- Two tbsp agave syrup (optional)
- Fresh mint leaves for garnishing (optional)

Directions:

1. In your big teapot, mix dried chamomile plus linden flowers.

2. In your medium saucepan, let spring water boil. Pour hot water on your dried flowers mixture. Let it steep within ten mins.

3. Strain into your cups. If desired, sweeten with agave syrup and garnish with fresh mint leaves before serving.

Nutritional Values (per serving): Calories: 30; Carbs: 7g; Fat: 0g; Protein: 0g

Cold & Flu Relief Burdock Root Tea

Preparation time: Ten mins

Cooking time: Twenty mins

Servings: Four

Ingredients:

- One cup fresh burdock root, thinly sliced
- Four cups spring water
- Two tbsp fresh lime juice
- One tbsp agave syrup (optional)
- One tsp sea salt

Directions:

1. Let four cups spring water boil in your medium saucepan. Carefully add burdock root, adjust to low temp, then simmer within twenty mins.

2. Strain into your teapot, then mix in lime juice, agave syrup (if using), plus sea salt. Serve.

Nutritional Values (per serving): Calories: 30; Carbs: 8g; Fat: 0g; Protein: 1g

Blood Pressure Regulating Hawthorn Berry Tea

Preparation time: Ten mins

Cooking time: Twenty-five mins

Servings: Four

Ingredients:

- One cup dried hawthorn berries
- Four cups spring water
- One tbsp dried sarsaparilla root, crushed
- One tbsp dried burdock root, crushed
- Two tbsp agave nectar (optional)

Directions:

1. In your big pot, mix hawthorn berries, sarsaparilla, plus burdock root. Add four cups spring water, then let it boil
2. Let it simmer within twenty mins. Remove your pot, then cool it down. Strain into your teapot, then mix in agave nectar, if desired. Serve.

Nutritional Values (per serving): Calories: 60; Carbs: 14g; Fat: 0g; Protein: 1g

Hormone-Balancing Red Raspberry Leaf Tea

Preparation time: Ten mins

Cooking time: Fifteen mins

Servings: Four

Ingredients:

- One cup red raspberry leaves, dried
- Four cups filtered water
- Two tbsp agave syrup (optional)
- One medium burdock root, sliced
- Two tsp sarsaparilla root powder
- One tbsp dried each elderberry flowers & blue vervain leaves
- One tbsp sea moss gel

Directions:

1. Mix red raspberry leaves, burdock root, sarsaparilla root powder, elderberry flowers, and blue vervain leaves in your big pot.
2. Pour four cups filtered water, then let it boil. Adjust to a simmer within fifteen mins. Remove your pot, then let it steep within ten mins.
3. Strain into your pitcher, then mix in agave syrup if desired. Mix in sea moss gel till fully dissolved. Serve.

Nutritional Values (per serving): Calories: 58; Carbs: 13g; Fat: 0g; Protein: 1g

Tips For Creating Your Own Alkaline Herb-Infused Meals

When it comes to adopting a healthy, alkaline diet, one of the crucial aspects is incorporating alkaline herbs into your meals. Alkaline herbs are known to help bring balance to the body's pH level, detoxify our system, and provide essential nutrients that support overall health and well-being. Let's explore some practical ways to make this transition easy and enjoyable.

1. Educate Yourself on Alkaline Herbs: Before starting with creating your own alkaline herb-infused meals, it's essential to learn about the different types of alkaline herbs. Some popular alkaline herbs include burdock root, dandelion leaf, elderberry, Irish moss, and sarsaparilla. Each herb boasts unique health benefits and can be prepared and consumed in various ways. You can start by researching the safety and uses of these herbs and consulting a health professional if you have any concerns or questions.

2. Create a List of Alkaline Herb-Infused Meal Ideas: To begin including alkaline herbs in your diet successfully, it helps to have a collection of meal ideas that incorporate these powerful plants' healing properties. Think about how you can incorporate them into breakfasts, salads, main dishes, and beverages in their most natural form to retain their nutrients.

3. Keep Your Pantry Stocked with Alkaline Herbs: To consistently implement an alkaline herb-infused diet, keep your pantry stocked with an array of your favorite herbs in various forms like fresh, dried, or powder. This will make it easier for you to create delicious and nutrient-dense meals at a moment's notice without the hassle of running out of essential ingredients.

4. Experiment with Different Cooking Techniques: When cooking with alkaline herbs, it's essential to experiment with different cooking techniques to maximize their benefits and flavors. Some alkaline herbs are best when consumed raw or steeped in teas, while others can be boiled, steamed, or sautéed. By trying various methods, you will be able to introduce a wide range of interesting flavors and textures into your meals.

5. Incorporate Alkaline Herbs into Existing Recipes: To make the transition easier, it's wise to start incorporating alkaline herbs into the recipes you already enjoy. For instance, you can add herbs such as cilantro, basil, or oregano to your favorite salad recipes or stir-fries for an alkalizing twist. Gradually increase the number of alkaline herbs in your cooking to get accustomed to their taste and reap their health benefits.

6. Grow Your Own Alkaline Herbs: Growing your own alkaline herbs not only allows you to have a fresh supply at hand but also ensures their quality and purity. Planting seeds in containers or your garden is relatively simple and a rewarding experience that can help enhance your connection with your food. Plus, by growing your own herbs, you know exactly where they come from and minimize exposure to harmful chemicals like pesticides.

7. Make Herbal Teas and Infusions: One popular way of incorporating alkaline herbs into your diet is by making teas and infusions. Herbal teas are not only a refreshing beverage option but also provide numerous therapeutic benefits. You can prepare an infusion by steeping fresh or dried herbs in hot water for several mins and then straining the liquid before consumption.

8. Seek Inspiration from Others: Look for inspiration from chefs, bloggers, and cookbooks dedicated to alkaline herb-based cuisine. You will find an abundance of resources online that offer creative and delicious recipes showcasing these nutrient-dense plants.

9. Listen to Your Body: Finally, as you start introducing alkaline herbs into your meals, listen to your body. Everybody is different, and what works for other people may not work for you. If a recipe or herb doesn't agree with you, it's crucial to acknowledge this and seek alternative options. Through trial and error, you can curate a plant-based menu tailored to suit your unique needs and preferences.

CRAFTING HERBAL PRODUCTS FOR HOME AND BODY

Herbal Products for Skincare, Haircare, and Home Cleaning

As we continue to explore the teachings of Dr. Sebi, it's essential to understand that his holistic approach not only applies to our diets but also how we take care of ourselves and maintain our homes. In this chapter, we will discuss herbal alternatives for skincare, haircare, and home cleaning that align with Dr. Sebi's teachings.

Herbal Products for Skincare

The skin, our body's largest organ, serves as a protective barrier between the external environment and our internal organs. Proper skincare is essential not only for maintaining a healthy appearance but also for overall health. In the world of natural healing, herbal products have proven their worth as effective remedies for numerous skin conditions.

The use of herbs and plants for skincare is an ancient practice that spans back to the earliest civilizations. Over time, people have discovered the great potential of these natural resources in nourishing, healing and rejuvenating the skin. Dr. Sebi's approach to skincare relies on incorporating plant-based products infused with powerful herbs that benefit the skin while avoiding chemicals and artificial compounds.

1. Burdock Root: Burdock root has anti-inflammatory and antibacterial properties that make it an excellent addition to any skincare routine. It aids in treating common skin issues such as acne, eczema, and psoriasis by reducing inflammation and promoting healthy cell growth. Applying a burdock root-infused oil or cream can help soothe irritated skin, remove toxins and balance oil production.

Burdock Root Soothing Oil

Ingredients:

- One cup of burdock root (dried and chopped)
- Two cups of cold-pressed olive oil or grapeseed oil

- One tbsp of dried rosemary
- One tbsp of dried lavender
- Half tbsp of dried calendula petals

Instructions:

1. In a clean and dry glass jar, mix chopped burdock root, rosemary, lavender, and calendula petals.
2. Pour the cold-pressed olive oil or grapeseed oil into the jar till all the plant materials are submerged.
3. Tightly seal the jar with a lid and shake it gently to mix the ingredients properly.
4. Store the jar in a cool, dark place for four weeks, making sure to shake it once every day.
5. After four weeks, strain the oil through a cheesecloth into another clean glass container, separating all the herbal materials from the infused oil.
6. Your Burdock Root Soothing Oil is now ready for use.

How to use: Gently massage a small amount of Burdock Root Soothing Oil onto your skin or scalp as needed for soothing relief. Store any remaining oil in a cool, dark place away from direct sunlight for optimal shelf life.

2. Sea Moss: Sea moss, also known as Irish moss or carrageenan, is a type of seaweed filled with vitamins, minerals, and antioxidants required for optimal skin health. Its gel-like consistency makes it ideal for use in natural skincare formulations like face masks, lotions or creams. Rich in antimicrobial properties, sea moss helps protect against irritation and infection while also deeply moisturizing and nourishing the skin.

Sea Moss Facial Mask

Ingredients:

- One fourth cup of sea moss gel
- One tsp of turmeric powder
- Two tbsp of raw honey
- One tbsp of freshly squeezed lemon juice

Instructions:

1. In a small bowl, mix sea moss gel, turmeric powder, raw honey, and freshly squeezed lemon juice.
2. Mix all ingredients together till well combined.

How to use: With clean hands or a spatula, apply a generous layer of the mask on your clean and dry face, avoiding the eye area. Leave the mask on for fifteen to twenty mins. Rinse off gently with warm water. Pat your skin dry and follow with your regular moisturizer.

Sea Moss Nourishing Moisturizer

Ingredients:

- One-fourth cup of soaked and blended sea moss gel
- One-fourth cup of raw shea butter
- One-eighth cup of cold-pressed jojoba oil
- Five drops of lavender essential oil

Instructions:

1. In a small saucepan, gently melt the shea butter over low heat. Once melted, remove from heat.
2. Carefully add the sea moss gel into the melted shea butter, stirring well to combine. Slowly pour in the cold-pressed jojoba oil, while continuing to stir the mixture.
3. Add five drops of lavender essential oil to the mixture for added fragrance and skin benefits.
4. Allow the mixture to cool down to room temperature before transferring it to a clean glass jar or container with an airtight seal.
5. Let the moisturizer set in the refrigerator for about two hours, or till it reaches a firm, creamy consistency.

How to use: Apply a small amount of Sea Moss Nourishing Moisturizer to cleansed skin, gently massaging in circular motions till fully absorbed. Use as needed for optimal hydration and skin nourishment. Store in a cool, dry place when not in use.

3. Calendula: Derived from marigold flowers, calendula oil works wonders for dry or irritated skin as well as minor wounds and burns due to its soothing anti-inflammatory properties. It helps reduce redness and swelling while promoting skin cell regeneration, making it particularly useful in treating conditions like eczema and dermatitis. Incorporate calendula into your skincare regimen through creams, balms or even a gentle toner infused with its healing properties.

Calendula Healing Cream

Ingredients:

- One cup of organic calendula petals

- Two cups of grapeseed oil
- Half cup of shea butter
- One tbsp of dried sea moss powder
- One tbsp of agave nectar

Instructions:

1. Begin by infusing the calendula petals with the grapeseed oil. Place the calendula petals in a glass jar, cover with grapeseed oil, and allow to sit in a sunny spot for two weeks, shaking occasionally.
2. After two weeks, strain the infused oil through a fine mesh strainer and discard the spent petals.
3. In a double boiler, gently heat the infused grapeseed oil and shea butter till the shea butter is completely melted.
4. Once melted, remove from heat, add the dried sea moss powder and agave nectar, and mix thoroughly.
5. Let the mixture cool for approximately thirty mins before transferring it to a clean glass container with a lid.
6. Allow the cream to cool completely before sealing and storing in a cool, dry place.

How to use: Apply a small amount of Calendula Healing Cream on affected areas as needed and rub in gently to soothe dry or irritated skin, minor wounds, burns, eczema, or dermatitis. Use within three months for optimal freshness.

Calendula Gentle Toner

Ingredients:

- Two tbsp of dried calendula petals
- One cup of boiling spring water
- One tbsp of raw apple cider vinegar
- Half tbsp of vegetable glycerin

Instructions:

1. Place the dried calendula petals in a heatproof container. Pour one cup of boiling spring water over the petals.
2. Allow the mixture to steep for twenty mins, then strain out the petals using a fine mesh strainer. Next, add one tbsp of raw apple cider vinegar to the strained liquid and stir well.
3. Add half tbsp of vegetable glycerin, stirring again to fully combine all the ingredients.

How to Use: Moisten a cotton pad or reusable facial cloth with the Calendula Gentle Toner and gently apply onto your face, avoiding contact with your eyes. Use this toner twice daily as part of your morning and evening skincare routine, after cleansing and before moisturizing. Store in a glass bottle and keep it refrigerated for best results. Make sure you shake the bottle well before each use.

4. Elderberry: Elderberries hold potent antiviral properties that help protect the skin from infections and strengthen the immune system. A natural antioxidant-rich herb, elderberry helps fight against free radicals, which are major contributors to premature aging and other skin issues. Elderberry can be added to skincare formulations like serums, face masks or moisturizers to revitalize the skin and improve its overall health.

Elderberry Antioxidant Serum

Ingredients:

- One-fourth cup of fresh elderberries
- One tbsp of cold-pressed olive oil
- One tbsp of raw, organic agave nectar
- Two tbsp of distilled water

Instructions:

1. Gently wash the elderberries to remove any dirt or debris.
2. In a small saucepan, heat the distilled water till it reaches a simmer. Add the elderberries to the simmering water and cook for ten mins, stirring occasionally.
3. After ten mins, remove the saucepan from heat and allow the elderberry mixture to cool completely.
4. Once cooled, strain the elderberry mixture through a fine-mesh sieve or cheesecloth to remove any seeds or solid particles, keeping only the liquid.
5. In a small mixing bowl or beaker, mix elderberry liquid, cold-pressed olive oil, and raw agave nectar. Whisk the ingredients together till well blended and smooth.

How to use: Apply a few drops of the Elderberry Antioxidant Serum onto clean fingertips and gently massage it into your face and neck daily, focusing on areas with signs of aging or discoloration. The serum works best when used after cleansing and toning but before applying moisturizer. For optimal results, use consistently as part of your daily skincare routine.

5. Sarsaparilla: Sarsaparilla, a powerful cleansing herb, is well-known for its blood-purifying properties. Its detoxifying effects on the body help clear the skin from impurities like acne and enhance overall complexion. It stimulates the production of collagen, improving both skin texture and elasticity while slowing down aging signs such as wrinkles and fine lines. Drinking sarsaparilla as a tea or incorporating it into topical creams allows you to experience its many benefits for your skin.

Sarsaparilla Collagen Cream

Ingredients:

- One-fourth cup of chopped sarsaparilla root
- One cup of shea butter
- Two-thirds cup of coconut oil
- Two tbsp of cold-pressed olive oil
- Ten drops of lavender essential oil

Instructions:

1. In a small saucepan, heat one cup of water over low heat. Add the chopped sarsaparilla root to the saucepan and let it simmer for twenty mins.
2. Carefully strain the sarsaparilla infusion into a heat-resistant container, and allow it to cool completely.
3. Place the shea butter and coconut oil into a double boiler, and heat them together till fully melted.
4. Carefully remove the melted mixture from heat, then add the cooled sarsaparilla infusion, stirring till well combined. Mix in the cold-pressed olive oil and lavender essential oil.
5. Transfer the mixture into a glass jar with an airtight lid, and let it cool down to room temperature. Store the cream in a cool, dark place.

How to use: Apply a small amount of the Sarsaparilla Collagen Cream to your clean face and neck in gentle circular motions twice daily, morning and night, focusing on areas with fine lines or uneven textures. Enjoy its revitalizing benefits for your skin!

6. Nettle: Nettle is rich in antioxidants, minerals, and vitamins that contribute to healthy glowing skin. It offers natural astringent properties that help tighten the skin and minimize enlarged pores as well as anti-inflammatory benefits that reduce redness and irritation caused by conditions like acne or eczema. Nettle leaves can be prepared as tea for internal consumption or used topically in creams or lotions for direct application.

Nettle Skin-Tightening Lotion

Ingredients:

- One cup of fresh nettle leaves
- Half cup of witch hazel
- One fourth cup of rose water
- Two tbsp of aloe vera gel
- Ten drops of lavender essential oil
- Five drops of rosemary essential oil

Instructions:

1. Rinse the nettle leaves thoroughly and pat them dry.
2. In a saucepan, bring a cup of water to a boil and add the nettle leaves to it. Simmer for ten mins and then strain the liquid into a glass jar, discarding the leaves.
3. To the nettle-infused water, add witch hazel and rose water, and mix well.
4. Add aloe vera gel, lavender essential oil, and rosemary essential oil to the mixture, stirring till all ingredients are combined.
5. Pour your lotion into an airtight container and let it cool to room temperature.

How to use: Clean your face with your regular cleanser. Apply a small amount of the Nettle Skin-Tightening Lotion on your face and neck with clean fingertips or a cotton pad, avoiding the eye area. Gently massage the lotion into your skin in circular motions till fully absorbed. Use this lotion twice daily (morning and evening) for best results.

Nettle Enlarged Pores Minimizer Cream

Ingredients:

- One cup of fresh nettle leaves
- Half cup of distilled water
- Quarter of a cup of pure aloe vera gel
- Two tbsp of grapeseed oil
- Ten drops of lavender essential oil

Instructions:

1. Rinse the fresh nettle leaves thoroughly and pat them dry using a clean towel.
2. In a small saucepan, add the distilled water and nettle leaves, then simmer on low heat for ten mins to create nettle tea. Remove the saucepan from heat and allow the nettle tea to cool down.
3. Once cooled, strain the liquid into a bowl, discarding the used nettle leaves.

4. Add the pure aloe vera gel, grapeseed oil, and lavender essential oil to the strained nettle tea and mix well till fully combined. Transfer the mixture to an airtight container to store.

How to use: Apply a small amount of cream on clean skin, focusing on areas with enlarged pores. Gently massage it into the skin using circular motions, allowing it to absorb completely before applying other skincare products or makeup. Use in the morning and evening for best results. Store in a cool, dark place away from direct sunlight to maintain effectiveness.

7. Yellow Dock: Yellow dock supports the body's natural detoxification process by purifying the blood and removing toxins that contribute to various skin disorders such as acne, psoriasis, eczema or rashes. Both its leaves and roots can be utilized in tinctures or topical applications like salves for soothing inflammation while promoting overall skin health.

Yellow Dock Detoxifying Salve

Ingredients:

- One & half cups of yellow dock root, chopped
- Two cups of organic coconut oil
- One-third cup of organic beeswax, grated
- Five drops of tea tree essential oil
- Seven drops of lavender essential oil

Instructions:

In a double boiler, gently heat the coconut oil over low heat. Add the chopped yellow dock root to the heated coconut oil and let it simmer for one hour, stirring occasionally.

After an hour, remove the double boiler from the heat and let the mixture cool for ten mins.

Use a fine-mesh strainer or cheesecloth to strain the yellow dock root-infused oil into a glass measuring cup or container, pressing firmly on the solids to extract as much oil as possible.

Discard the solids and clean the double boiler.

In the clean double boiler, mix infused oil with the grated beeswax and heat gently over low heat till completely melted and combined.

Remove from heat and let it cool for about two mins before adding tea tree and lavender essential oils, stirring well to ensure even distribution.

Pour the mixture into small glass jars or tins for storage while still warm, leaving enough space for expansion. Let the salve cool and solidify completely before putting on lids.

How to use: Apply the Yellow Dock Detoxifying Salve directly to affected areas, such as acne-prone spots, patches of eczema or psoriasis, or inflamed rashes, once or twice daily as needed. Allow it to absorb into your skin for optimal effectiveness in soothing inflammation and promoting detoxification.

Herbal products have much to offer in the realm of skincare. By embracing Dr. Sebi's teachings and incorporating herbs like burdock root, sea moss, calendula, elderberry, sarsaparilla, nettle and yellow dock into your daily routine, you can nurture your skin through safe and effective natural remedies. As always, it's essential to consult with a healthcare professional when introducing any new herbs or supplements to ensure they are suitable for your individual needs.

Herbal Products for Haircare

The beauty and vitality of our hair is often seen as a reflection of our overall health and well-being. As such, it's no surprise that many of us are continually on the lookout for effective and natural hair care solutions. The use of herbal products is not just a recent trend, but rather a practice that has been handed down through generations. This ancient wisdom is supported by scientific research, confirming the benefits of various herbs on hair growth, strength, and health.

Here are some essential herbal products recommended by Dr. Sebi for optimizing your hair care routine:

1. Aloe Vera Gel: A powerhouse in natural hair care, aloe vera possesses enzymes, minerals, vitamins, and amino acids that nourish the scalp and promote healthy hair growth. Its anti-inflammatory qualities help soothe irritation, reduce dandruff, promote blood circulation, and combat fungal growth on the scalp.

Ingredients:

- One large Aloe Vera leaf
- Two tbsp of cold-pressed olive oil
- One tbsp of freshly squeezed lemon juice
- Five drops of lavender essential oil

Instructions:

1. Wash the Aloe Vera leaf thoroughly to remove any dirt or debris. Carefully slice off the sides of the leaf to expose the gel within.
2. Use a spoon to scoop out the Aloe Vera gel into a clean glass bowl. Add two tbsp of cold-pressed olive oil and one tbsp of freshly squeezed lemon juice to the bowl.
3. Mix in five drops of lavender essential oil, which not only provides a pleasant scent but also has soothing properties for your scalp.
4. Using a whisk or hand mixer, blend all the ingredients well till you achieve a smooth and consistent texture.

How to use: Make sure your hair is clean and damp before application. Gently massage the Aloe Vera mixture onto your scalp and work it through to the ends of your hair. Once your entire head is covered, allow it to sit for thirty mins to an hour, enabling the nourishing properties to work their magic. Rinse thoroughly with lukewarm water, making sure to remove all residue from your hair. Allow your hair to air-dry for best results, and enjoy healthier, more radiant locks!

2. Burdock Root Oil: Rich in various nutrients like Omega-6 fatty acids, burdock root oil works wonders in promoting healthy hair growth by nourishing the scalp and improving blood circulation. Additionally, its antimicrobial properties guard against infections and scalp irritations.

Ingredients:

- One cup of burdock root (dried and chopped)
- Two cups of cold-pressed olive oil
- Ten drops of lavender essential oil
- Five drops of rosemary essential oil
- One glass jar with a lid

Instructions:

In the glass jar, mix dried and chopped burdock root with the cold-pressed olive oil.

Place the lid on the jar, then store it in a cool, dark place for two to three weeks. Gently shake the jar every other day to mix the ingredients thoroughly.

After two to three weeks, strain the oil through a fine mesh strainer or cheesecloth into another clean glass jar or bottle. Make sure to squeeze out any excess oil from the burdock root.

Add the lavender and rosemary essential oils to the infused burdock root oil, and mix well.

How to use: Apply a small amount of Dr. Sebi's Burdock Root Oil to your fingertips or palms, then gently massage it into your scalp and hair roots. Wait at least thirty mins or leave it overnight for a deep conditioning treatment. Wash your hair with your preferred Dr. Sebi-approved shampoo and conditioner as you normally would. Apply this Burdock Root Oil one to two times per week for optimal hair health and growth following Dr. Sebi Guidelines.

3. Lavender Essential Oil: Known for its soothing scent, lavender essential oil also offers numerous benefits to your hair health. Its anti-inflammatory properties help relieve an itchy or inflamed scalp while promoting blood flow and stimulating hair follicles to enhance growth.

Ingredients:

- Two tbsp of cold-pressed coconut oil
- Ten drops of pure lavender essential oil
- One tbsp of pure aloe vera gel

Instructions:

1. In a small glass bowl, mix cold-pressed coconut oil and pure lavender essential oil. Gently mix the oils using a wooden or silicone spatula.
2. Add the pure aloe vera gel to the mixture and continue to stir till thoroughly combined. Transfer the mixture to an airtight container or jar for storage.

How to use: Apply a small amount of the Easy Lavender Essential Oil Haircare mixture to your fingertips. Gently massage the mixture onto your scalp, working from the roots to the ends of your hair. Allow the mixture to sit on your hair for thirty mins, or cover with a shower cap for deeper penetration. Rinse your hair thoroughly with warm water followed by a Dr. Sebi-approved shampoo and conditioner. Use this haircare treatment once or twice a week for optimal results and hair nourishment.

4. Rosemary Essential Oil: An age-old remedy for hair growth, rosemary essential oil is believed to stimulate blood circulation to the scalp and nourish the hair follicles. Its antimicrobial properties also protect against scalp infections and dandruff.

Ingredients:

- One-fourth cup of cold-pressed olive oil
- Ten drops of pure rosemary essential oil
- Five drops of lavender essential oil (optional, for fragrance)

Instructions:

1. In a small glass container, mix cold-pressed olive oil with the rosemary essential oil. If desired, add five drops of lavender essential oil to enhance the fragrance.
2. Seal the container and gently shake it to mix all ingredients thoroughly. Store the mixture in a cool, dark place to preserve its potency.

How to use: Before using, shake the container gently to mix the ingredients. Apply a generous amount of the mixture directly onto your scalp and massage it for two to three mins. Leave it on your scalp for at least thirty mins or overnight (for better results), allowing the oils to penetrate your hair follicles and nourish them. After thirty mins or in the morning, wash your hair with a mild shampoo and let it air dry for optimal results. Use this treatment once or twice a week as part of your hair care routine to strengthen your hair, promote growth, and enjoy its invigorating scent.

5. Sage Tea: For centuries, sage tea has been used in hair care routines owing to its astringent properties that help cleanse the scalp of impurities and eliminate oily build-up. It also counteracts excessive hair shedding.

Ingredients:

- One cup of spring water
- Two tbsp of fresh sage leaves (chopped)

Instructions:

1. Bring one cup of spring water to a boil in a small pot. Add two tbsp of chopped fresh sage leaves to the boiling water.
2. Lower the heat and let it simmer for ten mins, allowing the sage to release its beneficial properties. Remove from heat and let the mixture cool down to a comfortable temperature.
3. Strain the tea into a jar or container, removing the sage leaves.

How to use: Shampoo your hair as usual and towel dry. Pour the cooled sage tea over your scalp and hair evenly, making sure to massage it thoroughly. Leave the sage tea on your scalp and hair for twenty mins. Rinse your hair with cool water, removing all traces of the sage tea.

6. Horsetail Extract: The silica content in this herb strengthens hair strands by promoting collagen production vital for maintaining the elasticity of our hair. Horsetail extract rejuvenates brittle or weak hair and enhances growth, giving you glossy and resilient locks.

Ingredients:

- One cup of distilled water
- Two tbsp of dried horsetail herb
- One tbsp of olive oil or jojoba oil (following Dr. Sebi Guidelines)
- Five to ten drops of lavender or rosemary essential oil (optional)

Instructions:

1. In a small pot, bring the distilled water to a boil. Once boiling, remove the pot from heat and add the dried horsetail herb. Cover the pot and let the mixture steep for twenty to thirty mins.
2. After steeping, strain the liquid into a clean jar or bottle, ensuring that all of the horsetail herb is removed.
3. Add the olive oil or jojoba oil to the strained liquid and mix well. Add the lavender or rosemary essential oil for additional scent and potential benefits.
4. Make sure the mixture is thoroughly combined before transferring it into a clean opaque container with a lid for storage.

How to use: Shake well before each use. Apply a small amount of the horsetail extract onto your scalp and hair, focusing on areas with thinning hair or breakage. Massage gently for a few mins to ensure even distribution and absorption. Leave it on for at least thirty mins or overnight for best results, then wash it off with your regular shampoo and conditioner following Dr. Sebi Guidelines. Use this treatment one to two times weekly for noticeable improvements in your hair's health and appearance.

7. Nettle Leaf Extract: Renowned for stimulating hair growth and fighting hair loss, nettle leaf is rich in vitamins A, C, K, and B as well as nutrients like iron and magnesium crucial for strong, healthy tresses.

Ingredients:

- One cup of fresh nettle leaves
- Two cups of alkaline water
- One tbsp of grapeseed oil

Instructions:

1. Thoroughly wash the fresh nettle leaves in running water to remove any dirt or debris.
2. In a medium-sized pot, bring the two cups of alkaline water to a boil. Add the washed nettle leaves to the boiling water and let it simmer for fifteen mins.
3. Carefully strain the liquid into a glass container, capturing the nettle leaf extract. Allow the extract to cool down to room temperature.

4. Once cooled, mix in one tbsp of grapeseed oil to create a nourishing haircare solution.

How to use: Gently massage the nettle leaf extract solution into your scalp and work it through your hair, ensuring that it is evenly distributed. Let it sit for at least twenty mins before rinsing it out with lukewarm water. Use this treatment twice a week for best results in promoting healthy hair growth and scalp rejuvenation.

Providing our hair with proper nutrition is just part of the journey towards lustrous and healthy tresses. Adopting a well-balanced diet, staying hydrated, minimizing heat styling, and avoiding harsh chemicals in hair care products are all essential contributors to your overall hair health.

Products For Home Cleaning

As we incorporate Dr. Sebi's herbal teachings into our lives, it is essential to understand that the concept of herbal healing does not merely apply to our physical bodies, but also to our environment. In this section, we will explore various natural and herbal products that you can use for home cleaning. These methods are sustainable, gentle on the environment, and help maintain the natural balance.

Herbal All-purpose Cleaner

Ingredients:

- 1 cup of distilled white vinegar
- 1 cup of water
- 20 drops of lavender essential oil
- 20 drops of tea tree essential oil

Instructions:

1. Combine all the ingredients in a spray bottle and shake well. Spray the solution onto surfaces and allow it to sit for a few moments.
2. Wipe clean with a soft cloth, sponge or microfiber towel.

Herbal Carpet Freshener

Ingredients:

- 2 cups of baking soda
- 30 drops of eucalyptus essential oil
- Pouring jar or shaker

Instructions:

1. Mix the baking soda and eucalyptus essential oil in a bowl thoroughly. Transfer it into a pouring jar or shaker
2. Vacuum your carpet to remove dirt, then sprinkle the mixture generously onto your carpet or rug. Allow it to sit for around one hour before vacuuming up the residue.

Herbal Window Cleaner

Ingredients:

- Two cups of distilled water
- Quarter cup of white vinegar
- Ten drops of lemon essential oil

Instructions:

1. Mix all the ingredients in a spray bottle and shake well. Spray the solution onto windows and glass surfaces.
2. Wipe clean with a squeegee, newspaper, or microfiber cloth for a streak-free finish.

Herbal Floor Cleaner

Ingredients:

- One gallon of warm water
- One cup of white vinegar
- 20 drops of peppermint essential oil

Instructions:

1. Mix warm water, white vinegar, and peppermint essential oil in a bucket or basin.
2. Dip the mop into the solution and wring out excess liquid before cleaning your floors. Allow your floors to air dry.

Herbal Disinfecting Spray

Ingredients:

- Two cups of water
- 10 drops of tea tree essential oil
- Five drops of eucalyptus essential oil
- Five drops of lavender essential oil

Instructions:

1. Combine all ingredients in a spray bottle and shake well before each use.

2. Spray onto surfaces such as countertops, door handles, light switches, and any other areas prone to germs. Wipe clean with a microfiber cloth or paper towel.

Eucalyptus-Mint Bathroom Cleaner

Ingredients:

- One cup baking soda
- Half cup liquid Castile soap
- Two tbsp white vinegar
- 20 drops eucalyptus essential oil
- 20 drops peppermint essential oil

Instructions:

1. In a mixing bowl, mix baking soda, liquid Castile soap, and vinegar. Then, add in the essential oils and stir well to create a thick paste.
2. Apply this cleaner to sinks, tiles, toilet bowls, and shower surfaces. Use a sponge or scrub brush to clean before rinsing thoroughly with water.

Herbal Laundry Soap

Ingredients:

- One cup unscented Castile soap (liquid or grated bar)
- One cup baking soda
- One cup washing soda
- Half cup white vinegar
- 40 drops lavender essential oil (or any other preferred scent)

Instructions:

1. In a large container, mix together Castile soap, baking soda, washing soda, and white vinegar till well combined. Add in your chosen essential oil and stir.
2. Use approximately one tbsp of this soap per load of laundry. Adjust the quantity based on your load size and individual preferences regarding scent.

By opting for these herbal alternatives over chemical-laden cleaning products, you are not only contributing to a greener environment but also protecting your health by reducing exposure to toxic substances commonly found in store-bought cleaners. Incorporating these recipes into your cleaning routine can lead to a more harmonious, balanced, and chemical-free home. Embrace the power of nature and reap the benefits of these all-natural, herbal cleaning solutions for maintaining a clean and healthy living environment.

Ensuring Safety and Effectiveness in Your Herbal Creations

The power of herbs in maintaining health and wellness is immense. Over the years, herbal medicine has played a significant role in curing various illnesses and promoting well-being. Let's explore how to ensure safety and effectiveness in your herbal creations to achieve optimal health benefits while minimizing potential risks.

1. Understanding the properties of each herb: The first step in creating safe and effective herbal remedies is understanding the properties of each herb you will be using. This entails knowing their medicinal qualities, potential side effects, and contraindications. Familiarize yourself with books, websites, and expert advice to gain comprehensive knowledge about each herb's attributes.

2. Sourcing quality herbs: The purity and potency of the herbs you use directly affect the safety and effectiveness of your herbal creations. Always source high-quality ingredients from reputable suppliers who maintain strict quality control standards. This ensures that your herbs are free of contaminants such as pesticides, heavy metals, or synthetic substances that might compromise their therapeutic value.

3. Following appropriate dosages: Correct dosing is crucial for ensuring safety in herbal medicine. While natural remedies have fewer side effects than pharmaceuticals, it is still possible to overdose on certain herbs or experience adverse reactions due to improper use. Consult experienced herbalists or refer to authoritative resources for recommended dosages specific to each herb.

4. Storing herbs properly: Proper storage is essential for preserving the potency and freshness of your herbs. To maintain their effectiveness over time, store them in cool, dark places away from direct sunlight, moisture, and heat sources. Use tightly-sealed containers made of materials such as glass or ceramic that prevent air exposure, thus preserving the herbs' aroma and quality.

5. Combining herbs knowledgeably: Herbs can have synergistic effects, meaning their combined use can result in greater therapeutic benefits. However, some herbs may also interact negatively, leading to undesirable consequences. When creating your herbal formulations, carefully consider the compatibility of herbs, their modes of action, and the possible outcomes of their combined use.

6. Adhering to cleanliness and safety precautions: When preparing your herbal creations, observe proper hygiene and safety precautions. This includes washing your hands thoroughly, using sterilized equipment and containers, and securing a clean workspace free of contaminants. Adhering to these guidelines minimizes the likelihood of introducing harmful substances or bacteria into your herbal formulations.

7. Conducting patch tests: Before using any new herbal creation on your skin, perform a patch test to check for potential allergies or sensitivities. Apply a small amount of the product to an inconspicuous area, such as behind your ear or inside your elbow. Wait for at least 24 hours to observe any signs of redness, swelling, or irritation. If you experience an adverse reaction, discontinue use immediately.

8. Keeping records: Documentation is vital for tracking progress and ensuring consistency in your herbal preparations. Keep records detailing each ingredient's source, quantity used, date of purchase or harvest, and any other pertinent information about the herbs incorporated into your creations. This aids in evaluating the effectiveness of specific formulations and identifying potential areas for improvement.

9. Staying informed about regulations: Ensure compliance with applicable laws and regulations governing the production and marketing of herbal products within your jurisdiction. Familiarize yourself with guidelines set forth by agencies such as the FDA or local health authorities that oversee safety standards for manufacturing practices and labeling requirements.

10. Continuing education: Lastly, commit yourself to continuous learning about herbal medicine and advancements in this field. Attend workshops, conferences, or online courses that enable you to stay abreast of current research findings while enhancing your knowledge and skills as a herbalist. This ensures that your herbal creations remain safe, effective, and in line with the latest scientific developments.

Adopting these practices will help you create herbal formulations that are not only safe and effective but also tailored to your or your clients' unique health needs. With diligence, patience, and understanding of the healing power of nature, you can harness the potent benefits of herbs and contribute to the ongoing legacy of Dr. Sebi's Herbal Bible.

Establishing a Daily Routine with Your Homemade Herbal Products

In this age of constant activity and stress, having a healthy body and mind is crucial to maintain balance. A daily routine incorporating Dr. Sebi's homemade herbal products can strengthen your immune system, enhance your overall health, and help center your mind. We will guide you on how to create your daily regimen.

Morning

Wake up to a fresh start by cleansing your digestive system. Prepare a glass of warm water infused with lemon juice or a tbsp of Dr. Sebi's approved apple cider vinegar to stimulate digestion, flush out toxins and give an energy boost. Sip on this elixir as you prepare for the day ahead.

Next, nourish your body with a herb-infused smoothie containing electric foods such as wild blueberries, frozen banana, strawberries, kale or spinach, soaked walnuts, and spring water. Blend these ingredients and add some sea moss gel or bladderwrack powder for additional benefits. Another power-packed morning meal option is an electric fruit salad with herbs like basil or mint and drizzled with agave syrup. Pair it with almond or coconut yogurt for added creaminess.

Mid-Morning

Stay hydrated throughout the day by sipping on refreshing herbal teas. Brew some burdock root, yellow dock root or dandelion tea to support kidney function:

- One tbsp burdock root powder
- One tbsp yellow dock root powder
- One tbsp dandelion root powder
- Four cups spring water

Boil the water and pour it over the herbs in your glass jar. Close, then let it steep within twenty mins before straining. Enjoy throughout the day.

Afternoon:

Lunchtime presents another opportunity for integrating healing herbs into your meal plan. Create nourishing salads filled with leafy greens, colorful vegetables, avocados drizzled with homemade dressing infused with Dr. Sebi's approved herbs like nettle, oregano, and thyme.

Alternatively, opt for vibrant soups like red lentil and vegetable soup with young coconut milk. Boost the flavor profile with herbs like cilantro, oregano, rosemary, and thyme.

Mid-Afternoon

When fatigue sets in during the afternoon, rather than reaching for sugar-laden snacks, energize with an herbal infusion like elderberry syrup or homemade ginger brew:

Ingredients:

- One cup dried elderberries
- Three cups spring water
- One cinnamon stick
- Half cup raw agave nectar

Instructions:

1. Mix elderberries, water, plus cinnamon stick in your saucepan.
2. Let it boil, then adjust to simmer till liquid reduces by half. Remove, cool it down, then strain. Mix in agave nectar, then store in your airtight container in your refrigerator.

Evening

Relax your body and mind as you wind down for the evening with a calming herbal tea made of chamomile or valerian root. These teas aid in better sleep quality. Dinner offers another chance to incorporate herbal products into your meals. Prepare alkaline grain bowls featuring vegetables like kale or arugula mixed with grains such as quinoa or wild rice coated in herb-based dressings or sauces like cilantro pesto.

Before Bed

Complete your daily routine with nighttime rituals that cater to your mental wellbeing. Spend a few mins journaling about the day while sipping on elderberry tea or simply unwinding with deep breathing exercises. Establishing your unique routine that incorporates Dr. Sebi's homemade herbal products may take some time but is undoubtedly worth the commitment. Your body and mind will thank you for the shift towards wellness as you embark on this journey of optimal health through nature's most powerful tools: herbs.

BUILDING A COMMUNITY AROUND HERBAL WELLNESS

Sharing Herbal Knowledge with Others

One of the most valuable and rewarding aspects of studying herbal medicine is sharing this knowledge. Dr. Sebi's Herbal Bible has introduced you to the world of herbal medicine and the incredible healing power of plants. As you continue to learn and grow on this journey, you may want to share this wisdom with your family, friends, and community. Why share herbal knowledge? Sharing herbal knowledge is crucial for several reasons:

1. Preservation: The more individuals who possess the wisdom that herbal remedies hold, the greater the likelihood that this information will withstand the test of time.

2. Empowerment: Equipping others with knowledge about natural remedies gives them control over their health, allowing them to make informed decisions and take responsibility for their well-being.

3. Helping the community: An informed and empowered community can work together towards better health outcomes and potentially reduce dependency on conventional medicine.

4. Keeping tradition alive: Herbalism is an ancient practice rooted in cultural traditions across the globe. Sharing this knowledge helps sustain and honor these long-established customs.

5. Environmental connection: Encouraging people to explore herbal remedies fosters a connection with nature as they recognize plants' therapeutic qualities and learn how holistic healing systems align with our bodies.

Sharing herbal knowledge with others doesn't require a formal education or qualifications – only a genuine passion for natural healing methods and dedication to passing on this invaluable information. Here are some ways you can disseminate herbal wisdom:

1. Teach classes or workshops: One of the best ways to share herbal knowledge is by teaching classes or workshops in your community. You can offer these classes through local schools, community centers, yoga studios, or even at home. Before teaching a class, ensure that you have a solid understanding of the topic you are covering and be prepared with helpful resources and hands-on activities for your students.

2. Start a study group: Gather a group of like-minded individuals who are interested in learning more about herbal medicine. You can meet regularly to discuss various aspects of plant medicine, share personal experiences, watch documentaries, read books together, and dive deeper into specific topics. Engaging with others who share your passion for herbs can be an enriching experience and help deepen your understanding of the subject matter.

3. Write articles or blog posts: Writing is another excellent way to share your knowledge with others. You can publish articles on websites or start your own blog dedicated to herbal medicine. Make sure to cite reliable sources to build credibility and support your arguments.

4. Share resources on social media: Use your social media platforms to disseminate valuable information about herbal medicine. Post links to informative articles, videos, podcasts, or books that resonate with you and may also be helpful to others.

5. Host plant walks: If you know about local plants in your area, consider hosting them to help others identify and learn about the plants around them. This is a great way to teach people about the medicinal properties of plants they may encounter daily. Always emphasize ethical harvesting practices and remain aware of potential plant misidentifications.

6. Create and share herbal remedies: When you have gained enough experience and confidence in working with herbs, consider creating natural remedies for your friends and family to try. This can be a wonderful opportunity to put your herbal knowledge into practice while offering thoughtful, handmade gifts that promote health and wellbeing.

7. Practice safe herbalism: Before sharing herbal knowledge with others, it is crucial to prioritize responsible herbal practice. Do not provide medical advice or diagnose illnesses, which may have legal implications and potentially harm others. Always inform individuals that they should consult a qualified healthcare provider before using herbs, especially if they have any pre-existing medical conditions or are taking medications.

8. Stay informed: As you share your knowledge with others, it is essential to stay informed about the latest research in herbal medicine to provide accurate information. Actively seek out new information and stay open to learning from reputable sources.

9. Encourage self-study: Encourage those around you who are interested in herbal medicine to study independently and consult reliable resources to learn more about herbs and their uses.

10. Be patient and humble: Sharing knowledge is a rewarding experience, but it is essential to remember that everyone learns at their own pace. Be patient with those around you who are taking the time to understand new concepts and respect their unique learning processes.

While it is crucial to share herbal wisdom with others, there are vital responsibilities to consider when teaching and guiding people in their herbal journey:

1. Present accurate information: Always do thorough research before sharing information – ensure that any claims you make are evidenced-based and well-substantiated.

2. Recognize your limitations: If you are unsure or unqualified to answer specific questions about herbs and health conditions, do not provide potentially harmful advice – instead, encourage individuals to consult with qualified professionals such as herbalists or naturopaths.

3. Empathize with individual needs: Understand that each person's health concerns differ – always approach conversations with sensitivity and respect their unique perspectives and needs.

4. Emphasize safety: Always stress the importance of using herbs responsibly – advise learners about contraindications, drug interactions, and potential side effects to avoid harm.

5. Encourage further education: Sharing herbal knowledge is only the starting point – encourage those you teach to pursue ongoing learning to make informed decisions and maximize their herbal skills.

As you continue exploring herbology, sharing your knowledge with others can be an immensely fulfilling endeavor. It allows you not only to deepen your understanding of the healing properties of plants but also offer valuable information that has the potential to impact the lives of others positively. Practicing responsible and safe herbalism, engaging in continuous learning, and sharing this knowledge through various means will strengthen the bond among those passionate about herbal medicine and contribute positively to the well-being of our communities.

Participating In Local Herb-Related Events

Herb-related events are gatherings where people share their knowledge, passion, and experiences with herbs and herbal medicine. These events can include workshops, seminars, conferences, markets, and festivals focusing on herbs' various uses, such as in food, medicine, cosmetics, and gardening. Participating in such events provides numerous benefits for those interested in Dr. Sebi's herbal practices or seeking a healthier lifestyle.

Benefits of Attending Herb-Related Events

1. **Expanding knowledge:** Attending local herb-related events will expose you to new information about the uses and properties of different herbs. You will learn about their

historical significance, cultivation methods, and applications in medicine and other industries.

2. **Networking opportunities:** Mixing with other herb enthusiasts will enable you to meet people who share your passion for herbal medicine. These connections may lead to opportunities for collaboration or learning from experts in the field.

3. **Supporting local businesses:** By attending herb-related events within your community, you are supporting small-scale farmers and businesses that produce and sell herbal products. This benefits the local economy and promotes sustainability by supporting eco-friendly practices.

4. **Discovering new herbs:** As you attend various events focused on Dr. Sebi's herbal practices or other herb-centric topics, you may come across unique or rare herbs that could benefit your health or enhance your repertoire of herbal remedies.

5. **Hands-on experience:** Some events offer workshops that provide hands-on experience in creating herbal concoctions, tinctures, and other plant-based remedies. This enables you to deepen your understanding of the process and learn practical skills that can be applied in your herbal practices.

Types of Herb-Related Events

1. **Herb walks:** A guided tour through a garden, park, or forest emphasizing the medicinal and edible plants found along the way. The walk leader will explain each plant's properties and uses while providing tips on identification and harvesting.

2. **Workshops and seminars:** Events focused on teaching techniques for incorporating medicinal herbs into daily life. Topics may include making herbal medicine, preparing natural cosmetics, or cooking with herbs.

3. **Conferences and symposiums:** Larger events centered around various aspects of herbalism. These conferences generally feature speakers, panel discussions, workshops, and vendors offering medicinal plants and related products.

4. **Plant swap meets:** Local gatherings where people exchange seeds, plants, cuttings, or advice on growing medicinal herbs.

5. **Farmers markets and herb fairs:** Events that showcase locally grown herbs and herbal products for sale. These events often feature stalls from regional growers and small businesses focusing on sustainable agriculture.

Tips for Getting the Most Out of Herb-Related Events

1. **Research beforehand:** Familiarize yourself with the event's program or workshop schedule to ensure you attend those most relevant to your interests.

2. **Take notes:** Bring a notebook or device for taking notes during presentations or workshops. Having written information will help you recall what you learned later.

3. **Connect with attendees:** Use the opportunity to engage with fellow herb enthusiasts. Share your experiences and learn from others in the field. Add new connections on social media platforms to stay in touch or join local herb groups to continue learning together.

4. **Support local artisans and businesses:** Purchase items from vendors at these events. Not only will this support sustainable, eco-friendly practices, but you'll also be adding to your herbal collection or finding unique gifts for loved ones.

5. **Apply what you've learned:** Once the event is over, incorporate your newfound knowledge and skills into your daily life. Whether trying a new recipe or concocting your first herbal remedy, putting theory into practice will help solidify your learning experience.

Nurturing The Next Generation of Herbalists

As we delve into nurturing the next generation of herbalists, it is crucial to understand that every effort and action taken today will leave an indelible impact on tomorrow's budding practitioners. From incorporating herbalism in early education to fostering a strong sense of community, this chapter provides a comprehensive roadmap for cultivating a thriving future for herbalists in sync with Dr. Sebi's teachings.

1. Incorporating Herbal Education in Schools: To foster an appreciation for herbal medicine among the young minds, schools must play an integral role by integrating lessons on medicinal plants into their curriculum. Encouraging students to learn about native herbs and flora around them pave the way for increased awareness and curiosity about their potential medicinal uses. This newfound knowledge will stimulate the children's interest to explore the field of herbalism, possibly leading some into professional careers later in life.

2. Building Young Herbalist Communities: Allowing young herbal enthusiasts to connect and share their passion is another essential aspect of nurturing future practitioners. Establishing clubs, online forums, or social media platforms that focus on sharing holistic recipes, remedies, or discussions specific to herbalism can foster camaraderie and a sense of belonging within this niche community. Encouraging mentorship from experienced herbalists can further inspire future generations as they hone their skills through guidance from their seasoned counterparts.

3. Hands-On Apprenticeship Programs: One cannot deny that practical exposure enables unparalleled learning windows – a concept equally applicable to budding herbalists-to-be. Facilitating apprenticeship programs under esteemed professionals' tutelage encourages young learners to observe, practice and comprehend the intricate methods of herbalism. From plant identification and cultivation to concocting remedial recipes, every opportunity given to eager learners will further nurture their capabilities as herbalists.

4. Promoting Ethical and Sustainable Approaches: A core principle in the teachings of Dr. Sebi is sustainability. This approach conserves the environment and ensures that future generations can rely on nature's bounty for healing. Imparting wisdom regarding ethical sourcing, fair trade practices, and conservation of medicinal plant species is as important as learning about their medicinal properties.

5. Networking Opportunities through Workshops and Conferences: Equipping herbalists with a wealth of knowledge from industry experts is another significant aspect in their development journey. Organizing workshops and conferences allows these aspiring professionals to build networks with celebrated practitioners, gather insights into innovative techniques, and remain informed about the latest trends in herbal remedies.

6. Inculcating a Holistic Lifestyle: Finally, committing to a lifestyle that embodies Dr. Sebi's principles is instrumental in shaping the future generation of herbalists. Young minds already delving into herbs' importance can benefit from following plant-based diets, detoxification protocols, and incorporating natural self-care practices in their daily routine. By adopting proper guidance that nurtures these potential practitioners' intrinsic abilities and passion, society can witness an emergence of well-rounded herbalists upholding Dr. Sebi's philosophy.

As we conclude this chapter, it is evident that sustaining Dr. Sebi's legacy lies in cultivating a genuine new generation of capable and dedicated herbalists. Such investment in our future has remarkable potential for unlocking healing secrets from the heart of Mother Nature. Embracing a wholistic approach while adhering to ethical guidelines safeguards the integrity of medicinal plants as time-tested healing sources. With each inspired young mind driven by curiosity to explore the world of herbal remedies, we take another step toward making Dr. Sebi's vision a reality. By igniting the passion for this ancient craft in our youth, we empower them to carry forth the baton as they embrace the path of healing, wellness, and harmony with nature.

CONCLUSION

As we conclude this read, the journey towards herbal wellness is far from over. This book has been a guide and resource, equipping you with knowledge and insight into the powerful world of natural healing. Dr. Sebi's approach to achieving optimal health through herbs may have been revolutionary during his time. Yet, it has become crucial to reclaiming control over our well-being in an increasingly toxic world.

With these teachings in hand, it is time to embark on your lifelong journey towards herbal wellness. From prevention and treatment of common ailments to overall detoxification and rejuvenation, you can harness the power of nature's apothecary to reinvigorate your body and mind. It will not be an overnight process, as true transformation often requires time and patience. However, by committing to incorporating herbal medicine into your daily routine, you set yourself on a path that will lead to greater well-being and longevity.

Reflecting on the Changes and Documenting Progress

As you begin to implement the lessons shared within this book and experience their effects firsthand, it is essential to note the subtle and profound changes that occur within your body. Whether you keep a journal or simply make a mental note, reflecting on these transformations will allow you to better understand your body's unique responses to Dr. Sebi's remedies.

Documenting your progress serves multiple purposes: it helps reinforce a sense of commitment while providing evidence of tangible benefits. As you celebrate small victories along your journey towards holistic health, maintaining a detailed account will empower you to remain consistent, track your progress over time, and inspire others who may wish to follow in your footsteps.

Building a Community of Support for a Herbal Lifestyle

Although pursuing a healthier life initially seems isolating, finding a supportive herbal community can provide significant encouragement and wisdom. Surrounding yourself with individuals who share your commitment to holistic wellness enables you to establish meaningful connections, exchange remedies and testimonials, and grow together as advocates of the herbal way of life. Communities can be found in-person and online through forums, workshops, and meet-up events for those seeking a deeper understanding of herbal healing. Investing in these relationships expands your network and enriches the continuous learning and exploration process that comes with adopting Dr. Sebi's teachings.

As we conclude, "The Dr. Sebi Herbal Bible" is not just a compendium of knowledge; it is a call to embrace a life-transforming journey. With dedication, practice, and support, you will continue to grow and share the invaluable teachings of Dr. Sebi. This book, your companion on this journey, invites you to pass on the torch of herbal wisdom. In the spirit of growth and community, we invite you to share your experience. If this book has touched your life, guided you on your path to wellness, or simply offered you a new perspective, consider leaving an honest review on Amazon. Your feedback not only helps us but also guides others who are seeking their path to holistic health.

Thank you for being a part of this journey. May the seeds of wellness sown through these pages flourish in your life and in the lives of those you touch.

APPENDICES

Glossary of Herbs and Terms

1. Alfalfa: A nutrient-dense herb containing several vitamins, minerals, and amino acids.
2. Aloe Vera: A plant known for its soothing and healing properties, often used to treat skin issues.
3. Anise: A sweet-tasting herb with a licorice-like flavor, used in cooking and herbal medicine.
4. Ashwagandha: An adaptogenic herb from India with benefits that include stress relief, improved immune function, low energy restoration, hormone balancing effects in men and women alike.
5. Bilberry: A close relative of the blueberry plant providing benefits related to eye health improvement and inflammation reduction while containing high levels of antioxidants.
6. Black Cohosh: Traditionally used to relieve menopause symptoms such as hot flashes and mood swings; some evidence supports black cohosh's ability to help balance hormones during menopause transitions.
7. Bladderwrack: A type of seaweed with high iodine content; often used in Dr. Sebi's herbal formulas for thyroid support.
8. Blue Vervain: A tall perennial herb that addresses nervous system conditions such as anxiety and stress relief.
9. Burdock: A herbal remedy used for detoxification and cleansing the body; also known for its anti-inflammatory properties.
10. Cacao: Raw chocolate beans with abundant antioxidants and essential minerals promoting overall health.
11. Cascara Sagrada: A natural laxative made from the bark of a specific tree species, used to cleanse the digestive system effectively.
12. Chervil is an aromatic herb rich in vitamins and minerals that supports kidney function.
13. Chickweed: A medicinal weed beneficial for skin conditions like eczema and psoriasis.
14. Calendula: A golden flower with antimicrobial, anti-inflammatory, and antiviral properties found in various herbal creams and ointments to promote skin healing.
15. Damiana: A Central American herb renowned for its purported aphrodisiac effects, also found to help improve mood and reduce anxiety or stress.
16. Dandelion: An edible plant with versatile herbal applications, known to support liver health and detoxification.
17. Elderberry: Antiviral berries believed to have immune-boosting properties.

18. Echinacea: This flowering plant's roots and flowers are widely used to help boost immune system function and fight infections, such as the common cold and influenza.

19. Fenugreek: Seeds of this herb are excellent sources of essential nutrients like iron, calcium, and vitamins that contribute to overall wellness.

20. Ginger: Root commonly used in herbal remedies for upset stomachs, nausea, inflammation, and pain relief.

21. Goldenseal Root: Anti-inflammatory herb traditionally applied for respiratory infections or an immune system booster.

22. Gotu Kola: Ancient Asian medicinal plant believed to promote mental clarity by improving brain function.

23. Ginkgo Biloba: Extract from the ancient Chinese Ginkgo tree improves blood circulation in the brain, deemed to enhance memory, cognitive function, and prevent age-related cognitive decline.

24. Horsetail: A medicinal plant with diverse health benefits such as strengthening bones, supporting hair growth, treating urinary issues, and promoting healthy skin.

25. Hawthorn Berry: Red fruit of the hawthorn tree, deemed effective against cardiovascular diseases, including heart failure.

26. Irish Moss: A seaweed hailed for its ability to promote digestive health effectively and nourish the skin, hair, and nails.

27. Kelp: A brown seaweed containing vitamins, minerals, and proteins that can assist with thyroid problems.

28. Lavender: A calming herbal remedy often used in teas, essential oils, and pillow sachets to relieve anxiety and enhance sleep.

29. Lemon Balm: An aromatic herb believed to alleviate stress, anxiety, and insomnia; also acts as a natural insect repellent.

30. Licorice Root: The sweet-tasting root is known not just for flavor but addresses gastrointestinal issues such as acid reflux, heartburn, and stomach ulcers with its anti-inflammatory benefits.

31. Mullein: Traditionally utilized for its anti-inflammatory properties to relieve respiratory ailments like a cough or bronchitis effectively by soothing inflammation in the airways.

32. Maca Root: Peruvian root plant linked to increasing stamina and combating hormonal imbalances.

33. Marshmallow Root: Herb known for soothing properties that relieve inflammation in the gastrointestinal system.

34. Milk Thistle: A herbal remedy used to detoxify the liver and prevent damage from environmental pollutants or medication overuse.

35. Nettle Leaf: Anti-inflammatory herb used for allergies, inflammation of tissues, or arthritic conditions; promotes overall wellness.
36. Oregano Oil: Potent antiviral properties offer immune system support by fighting off infections before they manifest into illnesses.
37. Pau D'Arco: An herb from South America with potential antifungal, antibacterial, and antiviral properties; sometimes incorporated as an immune system enhancer in herbal medicine.
38. Passionflower: Herbal treatment to address anxiety, insomnia, nervousness, or even muscle spasms while promoting relaxation.
39. Peppermint: Delivers relief from gas and indigestion discomforts while relaxing muscles in the gastrointestinal tract.
40. Red Clover: An herb rich in isoflavones helps maintain hormonal balance during menopause while offering other anti-inflammatory benefits too.
41. Rhubarb Root: Natural laxative derived from rhubarb plants helps detoxify the body by flushing impurities out of the digestive system effectively.
42. Rose Hips: Fruit of wild rose varieties rich in antioxidants like vitamin C that supports a strong immune system.
43. Red Raspberry Leaf: A nutrient-rich herb often used during pregnancy to tone uterus muscles while providing vitamin C, iron, calcium, forming part of an overall prenatal care regime.
44. Sarsaparilla: A tropical plant used in herbal remedies to improve digestion, detoxification processes, and overall immune health.
45. Saw Palmetto: Herbal remedy known for supporting prostate health while potentially reducing hair loss for males.
46. Sheep Sorrel: A herb known to have potent antioxidant activities that help eliminate toxins and reduce inflammation in the body.
47. Slippery Elm Bark: Herbal remedy used for digestive issues, notably soothing inflamed or irritated tissues in the digestive tract.
48. St. John's Wort: A herb widely known for its antidepressant and anti-anxiety effects, believed to have a positive impact on mood and overall well-being.
49. Turmeric: A potent anti-inflammatory and antioxidant, used as a culinary spice and herbal medicine for centuries, often incorporated in natural remedies for pain relief and inflammation reduction.
50. Valerian Root: An herb commonly prescribed as a natural remedy to combat sleep disorders, such as insomnia, while promoting relaxation and reducing anxiety.
51. White Willow Bark: Known as nature's aspirin, this herb contains salicin which offers anti-inflammatory, analgesic, and fever-reducing properties.

52. Witch Hazel: A plant with strong astringent and anti-inflammatory qualities frequently found in skincare products formulated to soothe irritated skin.

53. Yellow Dock Root: Herbal medicine used traditionally to purify the blood, improve digestion, and treat skin conditions such as psoriasis and eczema.

54. Yerba Mate: A South American herb offering rich sources of vitamins, minerals, polyphenols, and alkaloids known to assist in mental alertness, mood elevation, and weight management.

55. Yohimbe Bark: An African herb reputed for its potential role in enhancing male sexual performance by increasing blood flow; also used to improve energy levels.

Get Your <u>Free</u> Bonuses Now

BONUS #1: 5-Day Raw Reset Detox Plan

Jumpstart your journey to wellness with **a 5-day detox plan** designed to cleanse your body, reset your system, and boost your energy levels, all while staying true to Dr. Sebi's principles.

BONUS #2: Dr. Sebi Alkaline Cookbook

Delve into over **100 mouth-watering alkaline recipes** that not only adhere to the alkaline diet but also turn every meal into a healing, nutritious feast for your body.

BONUS #3: How to Get Protein Eating Green

Discover the secrets of **meeting your protein needs with plant-based sources**, ensuring your nutrition is holistic, sustainable, and perfectly aligned with an alkaline lifestyle.

References

1. Bowman, A. (2004). Dr. Sebi - The African Bio-Mineral Balance. Herbal Health Enterprises.

2. James, V. (2018). Dr. Sebi's Holistic Guide to Healing: Detoxifying the Body and Reversing Disease. Natural Healing Solutions.

3. Peters, K.L. (2020). Alkaline Plant-Based Diet Revisited: Dr. Sebi Approved Herbs and Recipes for Optimal Health. Wellness Publishing.

4. Morris, T.. (2016). A Guide to Dr. Sebi's Nutritional Guide: Using Electric Foods for Optimal Wellness and Alkalinity. Vibrant Health Solutions.

5. Thomas, G.R., & Wilson, J.S.. (2019). The Dr. Sebi Guide to Detoxification: Traditional Methods and Technologies of Healing with Herbs and Natural Foods – Path to an Alkaline Body Balance Environment. Self-Published.

6. Alexander, M.L.. (2017). A Journey through the Healing World of Dr. Sebi: Personal Experiences with Holistic Nutrition and Herbal Remedies.. Herbalife Publishing.

7. latitudeoflife.com/2018/02/dr-sebis-way-to-total-wellness/. Accessed 10 Jul 2022.

8. thealkalinediet.org/dr-sebis-5-powerful-recommendations-for-maintaining-healthy-ph-balance.html Accessed 14 Jul 2022.

9. dailydetoxhacks.com/dr-sebi-the-path-to-wellness/. Accessed 23 Jul 2022.

10. drsebiscellfood.com/approved-plants-fasting-detoxifying-and-alkalizing-body-healing/. Accessed 25 Jul 2022.

Made in the USA
Columbia, SC
26 August 2024

41090069R00074